SUCCESSFUL
SURGERY

◆

A Doctor's Mind-Body Guide
to Help You
Through Surgery

ROBERT W. BAKER, M.D.

◆

POCKET BOOKS

New York   London   Toronto   Sydney   Tokyo   Singapore

Human Nature Chart, p. 112, by George S. King, M.D. Copyright © 1934 by Medical Economics Company. Reprinted with permission from *Medical Economics* magazine.

POCKET BOOKS, a division of Simon & Schuster Inc.
1230 Avenue of the Americas, New York, NY 10020

Library of Congress Cataloging-in-Publication Data

Baker, Robert W., 1951–
    Successful surgery : a doctor's mind-body guide to help you
through surgery / Robert W. Baker.
        p.   cm.
    Includes bibliographical references.
    ISBN 0-671-51900-X
    1. Surgery—Psychological aspects.   2. Mental suggestion.
3. Autogenic training.   4. Surgery—Popular works.   I. Title.
RD31.7.B35   1996
617'.001'9—dc20   95-49049
                                                                                                                    CIP

First Pocket Books trade paperback printing May 1996

10   9   8   7   6   5   4   3   2   1

For Sheryl,
who got me started
and keeps me going

CONTENTS

◆

ACKNOWLEDGMENTS

◆

I am deeply grateful to all the people who played vital roles in the birth and development of this book.

Irv Settel, my agent: One evening, after I gave a public lecture, a man approached me and asked, "Have you ever thought of writing a book?" Yes, the notion had crossed my mind, but I had no idea how to go about getting it published. "I'm a literary agent," he said. "You write the book, and I'll handle the rest." Well, I did, and he did, and here we are.

Claire Zion, my editor at Pocket Books, with editorial assistance from Denise Silvestro: Their masterful application of just the right amounts of encouragement and discipline have allowed the writing to be fun, while keeping my excesses in check. Claire's editorial assistant, Danielle Dayen, was ever ready to answer even the silliest of my questions.

Kathleen Gebhart, C.M.I., Supervisor of Medical Illustration/Director of Media Services, Health Sciences Center, State University of New York at Stony Brook: Her immediate and thorough understanding of this project, along with her apparent ability to read my mind, enabled her to produce exactly the drawings I wanted with little help from me, the artistically challenged.

Ken Weber: a man of many careers with the talent to excel at all of them, my good friend's encouragement and suggestions were invaluable.

Medical colleagues: Several of my friends in the surgical specialties were kind enough to read the manuscript and offer their thoughtful insights. These included Henry Gardstein, M.D. (gynecology), Charles Libby, M.D. (urology), and Ira Udell, M.D., Associate Professor of Ophthalmology, Albert Einstein Medical College. I am especially grateful to Dan Reiner, M.D., Associate Professor of Clinical Surgery, Cornell University Medical College, and Michael W. Port, M.D., Attending Anesthesiologist, Huntington Hospital, Huntington, N.Y., for their early encouragement and their valuable suggestions.

My friends and medical partners David E. Cohen, M.D., Michael L. Cohen, M.D., Barry H. Cohen, M.D. (no, they're not related), and Jay Kugler, M.D., have been very supportive of this extracurricular activity.

My father, Leon C. Baker: the best writer I know, and the best writing teacher I ever had.

My greatest thanks must go to my family—my wife, Sheryl, and my children, Adam, Danielle, and Ashley—for whom, all too often, I have been the back of a head facing a computer screen. Their unfailing love and their understanding support of "Daddy's project" have been constant sources of motivation and strength.

Finally, I thank the many patients who have trusted me and tried the techniques in this book. Their own successful surgeries—and soon yours—are the greatest satisfaction this book has brought me.

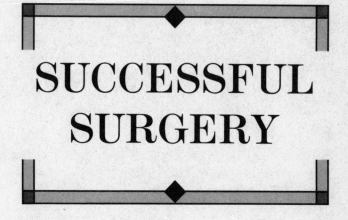

SUCCESSFUL
SURGERY

INTRODUCTION

◆

It's too late to turn back.

You've decided to take your doctor's advice and have the surgery. What you need now is a way to get through it as easily and painlessly as possible. This book will help you do that and more.

Successful Surgery will show you how to take advantage of recent advances in the burgeoning field of mind-body medicine to make your surgery and recovery as quick, comfortable, and easy as possible. If you're a bit skeptical, I understand. After all, probably the last three words anyone associates with an operation are *quick, comfortable,* and *easy.* But, believe it or not, you have the ability right now to make those words apply to your upcoming operation, whether it's a simple hernia repair or a coronary artery bypass.

The reason for this is simple: the brain is mightier than the scalpel. Using the power of your mind, your brain can enhance your body's ability to recover quickly from the effects of the

1

surgeon's knife. Did you know, for instance, that giving your body simple verbal instructions before surgery can significantly reduce how much blood you lose and lessen the chance you'll require a transfusion? Or that listening to a tape through headphones while under general anesthesia will lessen your need for pain medication during recovery? Or that it is possible with mental suggestions to improve your surgical outcome?

Such statements are not New Age flummery, nor are they "alternative medicine." They are supported by solid scientific research published in well-respected medical journals.

Remember that your brain influences, to a greater or lesser degree, *every* function in your body. There's a lot going on behind the scenes during those day-to-day experiences we take for granted—seeing friends, walking to the bus, tasting your lunch, feeling the pain of a cut. On an unconscious level, your brain is recognizing those friends and bringing up memories about them, recalling the route to the bus stop and monitoring the environment to get you safely there, deciding if the food is palatable and safe and then activating your digestive system to process and absorb nutrients, recognizing that an injury has taken place, mobilizing your immune system to fight off infection, and starting the healing process.

We have known for many years that the brain performs many vital functions on a subconscious level. What medical science is learning now is that it is possible to influence those functions *consciously*. This book will help you put the results of this research to practical use for your benefit. I have thoroughly searched the scientific medical literature to find the best techniques of mind-body medicine and have brought them together for the first time to help you sail through your surgery.

Let me tell you a fascinating true story about two patients from my own practice who dramatically illustrated the mind's ability to affect recovery from surgery.

Several years ago, two of my patients entered the same hospital on the same day planning to undergo the same operation by the same surgeon the following morning. Both of these women had been experiencing recurrent attacks of abdominal pain. One moment they would feel fine, and the next they would be seized by sharp, knifelike pain under their rib cages. These episodes could go on for hours, waxing and waning until finally the pain subsided.

When these patients had come to me for help, it was pretty clear from their symptoms what was ailing them, and a few simple diagnostic tests confirmed my diagnosis for each: diseased gall bladders full of stones. Equally clear was what needed to be done. They both needed surgery to have their gall bladders removed. It turned out that my two patients knew of the same surgeon and both wanted him to perform the operation.

Elizabeth was a seventy-five-year-old widow who went to work every day to run a successful clothing store she owned. She was all of five feet tall, weighed perhaps ninety pounds, and exercised every day. To keep her on my good side, I'll describe her as *feisty*. Elizabeth regarded her upcoming surgery as a temporary bother, to be gotten over with so she could get back to work. Now, this was before the days of laparoscopic "Band-Aid" surgery, where patients can go home the very next day after having their gall bladders removed. So I was concerned about how this "little old lady" would tolerate major abdominal surgery.

My other patient was Susan, a twenty-five-year-old who was also about five feet tall but weighed closer to 180 lbs. She was scared out of her mind at the prospect of undergoing an operation. I reassured her that she was young and healthy and would therefore have an excellent result and tolerate her surgery well.

Of course, I was wrong about both patients.

The morning following their entering the hospital, my friend Carl operated on Elizabeth and Susan one right after the other. Each procedure came off without a hitch, and each patient went to the recovery room in stable condition, as surgeons like to say.

Seventy-five-year-old Elizabeth left the hospital four days after her surgery and was back in her store a week after that. The day Elizabeth went back to work was the first day that Susan felt well enough to take a few steps in her hospital room. She had not had any specific complications, but her recuperation was slow and painful. Susan left the hospital three weeks to the day after her surgery and did not return to work for another month.

Two patients had the same operation by the same surgeon on the same day and had very different recoveries. Understand why, and you are starting to understand mind-body medicine.

I first really began to understand it some years ago when I used the mind-body technique of hypnosis to help a young woman who was about to undergo a major operation.

I had been using hypnosis for a number of years, but not for medical purposes. In college and medical school, I was a stage hypnotist, entertaining at hotels, resorts, and parties to earn money to help pay my expenses. I had hypnotized thousands of people. In my shows I often performed stunts in which the subjects seemed impervious to pain or demonstrated almost superhuman strength, and I often wondered if such mental abilities could be put to better use than making audiences laugh.

In medical school at the Columbia University College of Physicians and Surgeons, I took a course in medical hypnosis given by Dr. Herbert Spiegel, one of the leading hypnosis researchers in the world. Still, there was not much opportunity for a medical student to apply these skills to patients.

Then, during my postdoctoral fellowship at Harvard, my professor, Dr. Raj Goyal, took a great interest in my hypnosis skills and wondered if they could be applied to our own field of gastroenterology—the treatment of digestive problems. I suggested that certain potentially uncomfortable diagnostic procedures could possibly be done under hypnosis, especially with patients who could not tolerate the sedative medications we usually gave. Dr. Goyal urged me to learn everything I could about medical hypnosis, so I read more books and took more courses and started using hypnosis on patients.

At about this time, a very close friend of mine named Ellen found out that she required a fairly major operation. She would be under anesthesia for about three hours and was pretty anxious about the whole ordeal. I offered to help her lessen her anxiety with hypnosis, and she reluctantly agreed. Reluctantly, I guess, because she really did not "believe in" hypnosis.

In my courses, I had heard some stories about hypnotherapists giving suggestions to patients preparing for surgery that they would experience very little blood loss during their operations. At the time, there were few, if any, decent scientific studies proving that such suggestions actually had any effect, but I figured that giving them to Ellen during her hypnosis session couldn't hurt.

I had learned that a deep hypnotic state was generally needed to achieve the most dramatic results, but Ellen turned out *not* to be a particularly good hypnotic subject. She felt relaxed with hypnosis and afterward was less nervous about her date with the scalpel, but that was about all. During the hypnosis session, she actually snickered when I gave her the suggestions about decreased blood loss. Her reaction made me very glad I hadn't told her surgeon what I was up to.

The hours I spent with Ellen's husband waiting for the surgeon to give us a report were some of the longest I'd ever spent. The smile on the doctor's face when he came in swept away our fears. He told us that everything had gone extremely well, even better than he'd expected. I asked him casually, "Did she have much blood loss?"

"It's funny you asked that," he replied. "I don't remember the last time a patient having this operation lost as little blood as she did." Even with all my training, I was too dumbfounded to respond. After all, Ellen had not been a particularly willing hypnotic subject. She hadn't entered a deep hypnotic state. She really didn't put much faith in what I was doing. But the suggestions had worked! Ellen made a rapid, uneventful recovery.

Doctors have since learned that formal hypnosis is not necessary to achieve mind-body effects. You don't have to be very "hypnotizable" or suggestible. In fact, you can just think the words to yourself or have someone read them to you, and the power of the mind kicks in. All you need is to know what to do. I have shown many patients how to help themselves through surgery; I'd like to show you.

You have the capacity in you right now to affect very favorably the outcome of your surgery. You have the ability all by yourself to reduce pain without drugs. You have the wherewithal to speed your healing and recovery. You have the power right now to take control and to optimize your surgical result. The power is right there, *in your mind*.

Now let's unlock that power.

If you are having your surgery very soon—tomorrow, or even in the next few hours—please read Chapter 1 and then turn directly to Part III, "Emergency Surgery." Otherwise, please continue reading straight through the book.

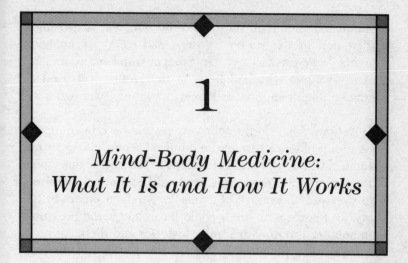

1

Mind-Body Medicine: What It Is and How It Works

The Olympic gymnast's face radiated the joy of his performance and betrayed none of the pain. His event was the rings, the purest test of strength and grace: a midair ballet demanding the most precise control over even the tiniest muscles. As his routine drew to a close, he catapulted himself into a series of midair somersaults, landing perfectly on his feet. Only the barest buckle of one leg, only the slightest wince, suggested that something might be amiss. As the audience cheered his performance, he collapsed into the arms of his teammates.

In the summer Olympic games of 1972, Mitsuo Tsukahara had won the Olympic bronze medal on the rings, completing his final event with a badly fractured leg.

At Stanford University, Dr. David Spiegel organized women with advanced breast cancer into two groups to study if those women who participated in support groups experienced less emotional trauma than those who did not. Not surprisingly, the women in the support groups had clear psychological benefits. Very surprisingly, Dr. Spiegel found ten years later that the women who had been in the groups had lived an average of eighteen months longer than those who had not.

Question: What do the following people have in common? (1) A group of more than three hundred senior citizens studied in California who had fewer trips to the doctor than some other seniors. (2) People in a study of heart attack survivors who survived an average of a year longer than others in the study. (3) People with lower cholesterols and blood pressures than another group with similar histories and diets.

Answer: The people who visited the doctor less or lived longer or had lower cholesterols all owned pets.

In England, researchers sprayed common-cold viruses into the noses of volunteers to study the body's ability to resist infections. Some of the experimental subjects developed symptoms of a cold and some remained healthy. The chance of a volunteer catching a cold was directly related to how much life stress he was experiencing at the time of the experiment. The greater the stress, the more likely he was to get sick.

These vignettes, ranging from the drama of Olympic competition to the everyday annoyance of the common cold, all share a common thread. Each demonstrates a remarkable connection between the mind and the body. Each reminds us that our minds and bodies are intimately linked in ways that affect how we respond to injury and illness.

Actually, you don't really need a reminder of the mind-body connection because you have experienced it many times in your life. When you were a kid, did you ever have an upset stomach the night before a big test in school? Playing golf, tennis, or baseball, did you ever "choke" when you let your nerves get the best of you? Have your palms ever grown sweaty watching a scary movie? On the positive side, has an aroma ever brought back a flood of pleasant memories? Have you ever felt energized just from stepping outside on a crisp autumn day? Of course you have. And we experience these things because our minds and bodies work in tandem.

In medicine, we have known of the mind-body connection for centuries. That's why a good physician knows that inquiring into a patient's lifestyle and everyday problems is as important as listening to his chest. The doctor also understands that her "bedside manner" is as much of a therapeutic tool as her scalpel or her prescription pad.

However, in trying to understand what causes illness, doctors have traditionally separated the mind from the body. For instance, if you caught a cold, it was because you were exposed to a virus. Your mind had nothing to do with it. With new research, this habit of separating the two is starting to break down, and we are beginning to study and understand how the mind and body interact in illness and health. Most important for you, we are learning how to put this knowledge to practical use.

Early medical reports on the mind-body relationship were simply observations. Patients whose hospital rooms looked out on a grassy scene recovered more quickly than those whose windows faced a brick wall. Angry cancer patients were more likely to recover than those who accepted their illness. At least thirty percent of the people participating in tests of a new drug would improve whether they received the new treatment or an identical-appearing placebo pill. These little whispers from nature all hinted that there was a major branch of medicine waiting to be explored.

Well, that exploration is going like gangbusters now, and reams of data are being published monthly. As with any new area of inquiry, the results of different studies sometimes contradict each other, and it can be hard to sort out what is significant from what is trivial. Sometimes the mass of information makes it hard to see the big picture: the old forest-versus-trees dilemma.

Since the purpose of this book is to help you use mind-body medicine, not to make you an expert in it, I'm not going to burden you with descriptions of scientific studies and analyses of data. *(You're welcome.)* But I do think that a simple understanding of how your mind and body interact will make the techniques you are going to learn that much more powerful and useful for you.

What Your Brain Is Up To

Your brain controls every function in your body, right?
Wrong.
A lot of what goes on inside you happens independently of your brain's authority. For instance, your white blood cells seek out and gobble up viruses and bacteria without waiting for instructions from upstairs. If you get cut, your blood starts to clot immediately without an executive order. Indeed, the complicated functions of your digestive system proceed very nicely, thank you, even if the organs' nerve connections to the brain are severed.

While the brain does not exert absolute control over these and other bodily processes, it can *influence* them. And since your brain and your mind are practically one and the same, your mind can influence them, too.

Generally, this influence occurs on a subconscious level; you are not aware of it. For example, I'll bet you've had the experience of glancing at a clock, noticing it's around noon, and suddenly feeling hungry. You weren't hungry the moment before you looked at that clock, but all of a sudden your stomach is churning, and your body is pleading to be fed. Why? Because your brain looked at the clock, saw the time, and thought to itself (*sub*consciously), "Twelve o'clock. That's usually lunchtime, which means that it's time to be fed. Well, if food is going to be delivered, I had better get the digestive juices flowing and that old stomach grinding. Yo! Crank it up down there! Food's comin'!" All of which translates into your being hungry.

Now, here's what's crucial for you and your upcoming surgery. What mind-body medicine teaches us is that, to a certain extent, these *subconscious* processes can be influenced *consciously*. You can actually learn to think commands to your body and affect body functions you thought were beyond your conscious reach. In this way, you can lessen blood loss, speed recovery, etc.

If you doubt that you can learn to control subconscious processes, let me remind you that you've already done this at least once that I know of. When you were a baby, you had absolutely no conscious control over the emptying of your bladder. When your bladder was full, it sent a message to your brain to let it know. Your brain responded by allowing a little muscle at the bottom of your bladder to relax. Consequence: wet diaper.

Sooner or later, some parental authority figure impressed on your conscious mind that wet diapers were no longer socially acceptable. A crucial learning link developed by which your conscious mind began to recognize the subconscious signals that your bladder was sending up. In addition, your brain figured out a way to control that little bladder muscle and make it stay clamped shut until it received a direct *conscious* order to relax and let the urine out.

Fortunately, the techniques of mind-body medicine you are going to learn are a heck of a lot easier to master than toilet training!

If you can learn to consciously manipulate a fairly mundane body process such as urination, what about other, more obscure functions? Can you consciously control where in your body your blood flows? Can you make yourself feel less pain? Can you direct your body to heal faster or fight infections more efficiently?

Let's consider that last question by examining your immune system—made up of your body's defense forces. The immune system's complex army of billions of white blood cells roams your body, seeking out and destroying invading viruses and bacteria. The immune system may also identify and eliminate body cells that turn cancerous.

As I mentioned earlier, all this seems to happen quite independently of the brain's control, and people never thought much about the mind's influence over the immune system. Now, however, scientific evidence indicates that the brain does play a role in modulating the immune system. I know I promised not to burden you with discussions of scientific papers, but this story is too good to pass up.

Pavlov and You

Remember Pavlov's dogs? To remind you, Ivan Petrovich Pavlov, a Russian physiologist, discovered what he called conditioned reflexes. He would show dogs a piece of meat when he rang a bell. At the sight of the meat, the dogs would start to salivate. After Pavlov did this several times, he rang the bell without showing the dogs the meat. They would start to salivate all the same, just from the sound of the bell.

Normally, salivation at the sight of meat is a reflex, a function not under conscious control. Pavlov showed that you could change a reflex, or condition it, to respond to something other than its normal stimulus.

A hundred years later, Robert Ader, an American physiologist, was studying conditioned reflexes in rats. He gave rats a saccharine-and-water mixture to drink and at the same time injected them with a small amount of a drug that causes nausea. The idea was to condition the rats to associate the sweet mixture with nausea so that they would avoid drinking the saccharine water.

Dr. Ader had difficulty with his research, though, because the rats kept getting infections and dying on him before completing the experiment. Ader knew that the nausea-producing drug he had used also briefly suppressed the rats' immune systems. The drug did this by reducing the number of T-cells, a kind of white blood cell. However, the rats had received only one small dose of the drug—enough to teach them to avoid the sweet water, but not enough to make them permanently vulnerable to infection.

Then Dr. Ader had a brilliant idea. He thought that perhaps he had conditioned more than the rats' behavior by teaching them to avoid saccharine water. Perhaps he had also conditioned them to suppress their immune systems in response to the sweet taste. Maybe the rats were dying because every time they drank the saccharine water they suppressed their immune systems. Sure enough, further experiments revealed that when rats were given saccharine water weeks after their initial exposure, the number of their disease-fighting T-cells fell.

Just as Pavlov's dogs had salivated to the bell, Ader's rats suppressed their immune systems in response to saccharine water. Somehow, the brain had learned to respond to the sweet taste by suppressing the immune system. Here was the first experimental evidence of a connection between the brain and the immune system. (Subsequently, Canadian researcher Reginald Gercynski demonstrated that one could similarly condition animals to *enhance* rather than suppress their immune function. This knowledge will be helpful to us later.)

How can the mind affect the response of the immune system? How can the brain, sitting way up there in the cranium, affect tiny white blood cells way down in the little toe? It turns out that the body's internal communication network is much more complicated than anybody ever thought, and the brain can indeed influence even the most remote function.

You probably know that your brain communicates with your body primarily through your nervous system. Think of the nerves as tiny electrical wires that originate in the brain, leave the skull through the spinal cord, and fan out to the farthest reaches of your body. (*Figure 1*)

Some nerves carry information up to your brain, such as the soft feel of your cat's fur as you stroke her. Other nerves transmit orders down from the brain, to direct your hand and finger muscles to scratch under your cat's ears. Every muscle and every organ in your body has nerve connections to the brain over which constant two-way communication takes place.

As proficient as your nervous system is at its tasks, your brain also relies on your endocrine system to regulate body functions. This collection of glands—adrenal, thyroid, pituitary, and others—do their jobs by secreting messenger proteins, or hormones, into the bloodstream. The blood whisks the hormones to targets throughout the body. In *Figure 2*, some of the glands have been added to the diagram.

Notice that there are nerves to carry messages from the brain right to the glands. For instance, when your brain recognizes danger, it shoots a message down the nerves to the adrenal glands to secrete the hormone epinephrine (or adrenaline) into the blood. The blood carries the epinephrine to the heart, where the hormone causes the heart to beat faster in preparation for defending you.

Many organs also have their own hormones that work locally. For instance, the stomach secretes a hormone that makes it produce acid to digest food. The dozens of hormones in you make you grow, regulate your energy consumption, assist digestion, control the flow of fluids into and out of your body, and perform a myriad of other essential tasks. Some hormones even affect the cells of your immune system.

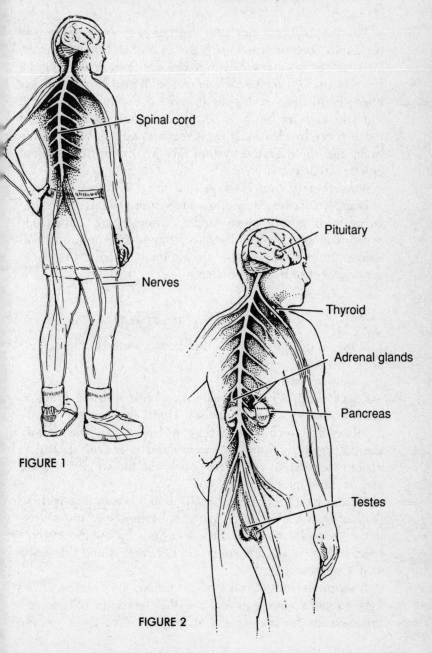

Spinal cord

Nerves

FIGURE 1

Pituitary

Thyroid

Adrenal glands

Pancreas

Testes

FIGURE 2

These local hormones may also play a crucial role in how the brain communicates with the rest of the body. Certain areas of the brain respond to hormones from distant organs. For instance, that stomach hormone I just mentioned has been found deep in the brain, where the hormone would seem to have no business being. Of course, nature did not put it there by chance. It must serve some link between the brain and the digestive system. We just haven't figured out exactly what that is yet.

Nevertheless, here is the crucial point. The brain, nervous system, endocrine glands, immune system, and hormones are far more complexly intertwined and overlapping than anyone ever imagined. The connections all appear to be in place to enable the brain, and therefore the mind, to affect just about every aspect of bodily function.

Do Try This at Home

Want to experience the mind-body connection in action? Give this a try:

Please salivate.

That's right. Give your salivary glands a direct order to start producing saliva. Go ahead. Do it. Right now.

I'll bet not much is happening. At least not in your salivary glands. Probably your conscious mind is actively trying to decide whether to throw this book out the window. Before you do, read on a bit.

Here is a different route to salivation, via your imagination. (Either read the following paragraphs *slowly* to yourself or, better, have someone read them to you. Follow the instructions and try to see and smell and taste everything I describe as if it were real.)

Imagine in front of you a bright yellow, juicy lemon. If you have to, close your eyes and see that lemon in your mind's eye. See the lemon as big and bright yellow. Even see the details of the lemon—its rough surface and the spot where someone stamped SUNKIST on the skin.

Now hold that imaginary lemon up to your nose. Inhale deeply, and imagine you can smell the lemony scent. Really smell it. Close your eyes, and in your mind hold that bright yellow lemon right under your nose. Feel the coolness of its skin against yours. Inhale that scent. Take a deep breath and smell that lemon.

Imagine now that you are peeling that lemon open. As you do so, the scent of the lemon intensifies. See the pulp of the lemon beneath the skin. Look at it for a moment and see that shiny lemon pulp. Now take a bite out of that lemon. Actually open your mouth and taste that lemon as you bite down. Taste that lemony, tart taste. Feel the juice flowing over your tongue. Taste it. Smell it. Taste the lemon.

Notice anything? Feel the saliva going? Now you understand how the conscious mind can influence the body. And you also see that the approach often needs to be a bit oblique. It is rare that we can simply address subconscious processes directly and expect the body to listen, though it does happen. Usually, you have to use indirect techniques that employ subconscious mechanisms such as imaging and suggestion.

By the way, if you did not start salivating to the imaginary lemon, don't worry. You still have all the ability you need to use mind-body techniques to help you through surgery. Remember, not everyone has the athletic talent to play baseball like Joe DiMaggio, but anyone can learn to play catch.

Now that you know a bit about mind-body medicine and techniques, I must tell you that we have only scratched the surface. There are many aspects of this new area of inquiry that are fascinating but beyond the scope of this book. I have not discussed meditation, hypnosis, self-relaxation, and related practices, though you will be using them. I have not tried to summarize the research on your emotions' role in your health, but you will be marshaling positive feelings to help you through. I have barely touched on the role of social support, though your friends and family will be great helpers. I hope that you will want to learn more about mind-body medicine and that when you have some time after your surgery, you will check into some of the books listed in Part V, "Resources," for further reading.

For right now, remember these points: your mind-body connection is there and waiting to serve you. Everything required to help you sail through surgery is already inside you. The techniques you are about to learn are easy, pleasant, and even fun. They cannot hurt you.

Now all you need to do is relax, read, and learn. Your mind will do the rest.

I

PREPARATION FOR SURGERY:
What You Bring to the Table

◆

The objective of your preparation for surgery was laid out in the first century A.D. by the Roman poet Juvenal:

Mens sana in corpore sano.

(A sound mind in a sound body.)

Pretty good advice from a guy who probably wasn't conversant with modern surgical techniques.

It doesn't matter whether you are young or old, heavy or thin, active or immobile, athletic or more like me. The goal is the same: to get yourself in the best shape—mentally and physically—you can.

What's important here are the words *you can*. Getting in shape is a very individual thing. Some folks will have the time and ability to put a lot of effort into getting ready for surgery. You may not. It doesn't matter. Anything you do to prepare yourself will be helpful. And it will be fun.

Come again?

Yes. Getting ready for surgery is remarkably easy, and it's

fun. You'll need to learn some mental exercises to reduce stress and strengthen your mind-body connection. As you are about to find out in Chapter 2, the exercises are extremely easy to learn and very enjoyable to do. They'll make you feel good!

Also to help prepare your mind, you should be familiar with what you are going to experience before, during, and after your surgery. Studies have shown that people who know in advance the details of what they will actually experience—right down to the sights, sounds, and sensations of surgery—generally have better outcomes. That's what Chapter 3 covers. Of course, surgical practices differ from hospital to hospital, but there are enough common elements that I can give you a pretty good picture of just what is going to happen.

Some of my patients say, "I don't want to know; just let them do their thing." Frankly, this is the attitude of many older patients, people who were brought up in the "doctor knows best" days. Let me remind anyone who might have such thoughts, for even a fleeting moment, of what Francis Bacon said four hundred years ago: "Knowledge is power."

In Chapter 4 we'll discuss how to share control with your surgeon and the hospital staff. Remember, your surgery is not a you-versus-them battle, but a cooperative effort. However, at the risk of offending some of my colleagues, I'll say that surgeons as a group are not necessarily people who easily share control. Also, nurses and other hospital personnel are sometimes too overwhelmed with work to change time-honored routines. So we'll spend some time on how to enlist the cooperation of all the professionals who will be helping to take care of you in the hospital. You'll learn how to be a "good patient"—which is not to say a passive one—whom everyone wants to help.

While readying your mind, you shouldn't neglect your body. You probably need to eat a bit more healthily. No problem. The dietary recommendations in Chapter 5 are scientifically sound and easy to follow. Getting your heart and lungs in better shape for your operation is also a good idea. In Chapter 5 I'll also outline an exercise program for people who hate to exercise.

Whether you have a few weeks, a few days, or only a few hours to get ready for surgery, you can help yourself greatly. All you have to do is decide that *you can*.

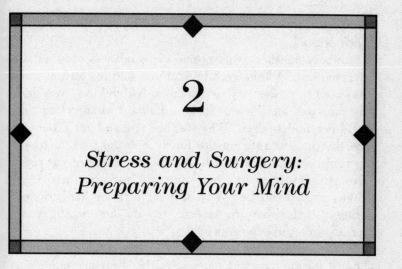

2

Stress and Surgery: Preparing Your Mind

No one likes surgery.

The fact is that most people regard surgery as a sometimes necessary evil, best to be avoided. So it doesn't surprise me that more often than not, when my patients learn that they need surgery, one of the first questions they ask me is, "Isn't there some other treatment?" Or, "Can't we try medication first?" Like *My Fair Lady*'s Henry Higgins, they "would prefer a new edition of the Spanish Inquisition than to ever let a" surgeon into their lives.

Recently, I had a startlingly dramatic demonstration of this sentiment. A man came to see me with a several-month history of abdominal pain, difficulty eating, and weight loss. Unfortunately, he turned out to have stomach cancer that had spread throughout his abdomen. The cancer was too far advanced to operate, and I told him this as gently as I could. His response: "Thank God. I thought you were going to tell me I needed surgery!" I was profoundly struck by the fact

23

that this man would rather face incurable cancer than a surgeon's scalpel.

Similarly, another patient came to my office because he was "stressed out." I knew that he had just sold his business and was about to retire very comfortably. His children were happily married, and he was looking forward to spending time with his grandchildren. Why was he "stressed out"? Because now that he was retiring, he finally had the time to have a hip replacement done that he had been putting off for years. "Everything was going great," he said, "and now this."

Why should this be? Why do people try so hard to avoid surgery? If they have to have it, why do they regard it as a terribly stressful experience?

On the surface, the answer seems pretty obvious. But think about it for a moment. Chances are that your upcoming surgery is going help solve a serious medical problem you have. When the surgery's all done you'll most likely be better off than you are right now. That uncomfortable hernia will be gone; that crippling arthritic hip will be fixed; that tumor will be removed; those blocked blood vessels will be opened. Your surgery is going to help you to live longer or better.

So why do we all hate the idea of having surgery? The answer is simple: because of the things we fear may happen to us. We fear that something will go wrong with the anesthesia and that we will "never wake up." We fear that the surgeon may make a mistake. We fear that we will hurt and will have to lie there in bed in pain until a nurse gets around to giving us medication. We fear a lengthy recovery during which we will not be able to care for ourselves. We fear that our jobs, families, and lives will be disrupted.

Do you see the common thread that runs through all these fears? In each, what happens to us seems completely in the hands of other people. Each situation seems entirely out of our control, and one of the things people find most stressful and fear most is a loss of control.

All of us like to feel in control of our lives. In reality, we know that there are lots of things we can't control: the traffic jam that makes us late to work, the rain that ruins a family picnic, the teenager with an attitude. But even with these stressors we try to find some way to gain control: we take another route, we plan a rain date, we ground the kid.

But with surgery, we don't see any opportunity for control. My patients say, "What can I do? I'll be asleep the whole time." Or, "You just lie there like a slab of meat and they work on you."

Wrong. WRONG. *WRONG!*

You are as active a participant in your surgery as the doctors, nurses, and operating room personnel. You have as much ability to influence the outcome as they do. You just don't know how to yet.

The purpose of the next four chapters is to show you what makes surgery a potentially stressful, unpleasant experience and teach you a number of ways to make your surgical experience as stress-free, as successful, and—dare I say it—as pleasant as possible.

First, in the remainder of this chapter, you'll learn what makes stress stressful. As elementary as that may seem, stress is actually an extensively studied and well-understood phenomenon, and gaining a greater insight into the mechanisms of stress will greatly help you to reduce it. You will also learn some simple, enjoyable stress-reducing exercises to start doing right away to lower your anxiety about surgery and start to strengthen your mind-body connection.

Then, in the following chapters, you will learn what you are going to experience in the hospital, how to forge a strong relationship with your surgeon and the hospital staff, and how to prepare your body for surgery.

What you want to bring to the table (the operating room table, that is) is knowledge, confidence, freedom from stress, and fitness of mind and body. Let's go get 'em.

Surgery, Stress, and You

THE HARM OF STRESS

The reason you need to learn to reduce stress is not just so that you'll feel better. Scientific evidence suggests that stress can have a direct, harmful effect on the outcome of your surgery.

Dr. Bernard S. Linn and his colleagues from the University of Miami examined the effects of stressful life events on the surgical outcomes of a group of healthy men having hernias repaired. Patients whose lives had been stressful for the six months prior to surgery had more complications, required more pain medication, and had slower recoveries than those men who had not had as much stress.

You may be thinking, "Well, up till now, I haven't had that much stress in my life, so I shouldn't have to worry about how stress affects my surgical outcome." However, you may have had more stress than you realize, and you cannot ignore the stress of the surgery itself.

In a classic study of stress in the 1960s, Drs. Thomas Holmes and Richard Rahe developed a list of forty-three life events and asked hundreds of people to rate the amount of stress they associated with each one. Marriage was arbitrarily assigned fifty points, and the study participants gave numerical values to the other events as compared to marriage. The results are shown in the following table:

THE HOLMES-RAHE SCALE

1.	Death of a spouse	100
2.	Divorce	73
3.	Marital separation	65
4.	Jail term	63
5.	Death of a close family member	63

6. Personal injury or illness 53
7. Marriage 50
8. Fired from work 47
9. Marital reconciliation 45
10. Retirement 45
11. Change in family member's health 44
12. Pregnancy 40
13. Sexual difficulties 39
14. Gain of new family member 39
15. Business readjustment 39
16. Change in financial state 38
17. Death of close friend 37
18. Change to different line of work 36
19. Change in number of arguments w/spouse 35
20. Mortgage over $10,000 [1960 dollars] 31
21. Foreclosure of mortgage or loan 30
22. Change in responsibilities at work 29
23. Son or daughter leaving home 29
24. Trouble with in-laws 29
25. Outstanding personal achievement 28
26. Wife begin or stop work [1960s!] 26
27. Begin or end school 26
28. Change in living conditions 25
29. Revision of personal habits 24
30. Trouble with boss 23
31. Change in work hours or conditions 20
32. Change in residence 20
33. Change in schools 20
34. Change in recreation 19
35. Change in church activities 19
36. Change in social activities 18
37. Mortgage or loan less than $10,000 [1960 dollars] 17
38. Change in sleeping habits 16
39. Change in number of family get-togethers 15
40. Change in eating habits 15
41. Vacation 13
42. Christmas 12
43. Minor violations of the law 11

Using this list, Holmes and Rahe demonstrated that the more stress in a person's life, the greater the risk that he or she will develop a serious illness. In other words, stress seemed to have a direct adverse effect on people's health.

Notice that number six on the list was personal injury or illness (including surgery). Surgery itself is a very stressful event. In fact, as you look over the list, you may identify several other recent events in your life that could add to the stress the anticipation of your surgery might be causing you. All of these stresses can affect your surgical outcome adversely.

One of the ways stress influences your health is by weakening your immune system, making you more susceptible to infections. This is why the researchers in England that I mentioned at the beginning of Chapter 1 found that people under stress were more likely to get sick when exposed to cold viruses. More important than whether you are likely to get a cold, however, is whether you are at risk for getting an infection after surgery—one complication everyone very much wants to avoid.

Just how stress directly affects the immune system is the subject of much ongoing research. Drs. Janice K. Kiecolt-Glaser and Ronald Glaser, at Ohio State University, have studied the immune systems of medical students (researchers' favorite guinea pigs) when the students were experiencing the stress of taking exams. During the exam period, the Glasers found that certain white blood cells that normally kill off viruses were less active in the students than they were when the students were not under stress. During stress the students produced up to ninety percent less of a certain chemical that stimulates those cells to activity.

What is particularly significant for our purposes is that the Glasers also discovered that teaching the students the type of self-relaxation exercises you are about to learn eliminated the negative effects of stress on the immune system functions being tested.

That's one of the things this book will help you do. By reducing stress, you will be enabling your immune system to function at its normal level, and you will be reducing your risk for postoperative complications. At the very least, by lessening your stress you are going to feel a whole lot better.

UNDERSTANDING STRESS

You don't have to be an expert to know what stress is; you experience it every day. But if I asked you to give me a concise definition of *stress*, you might have some difficulty. The reason it's so hard to define stress is that the word has taken on a broad range of meanings. When some people discuss stress, they are referring to the pressures the world is subjecting them to. Other people mean the feelings of tension they have because of those pressures.

When scientists use the term *stress*, they mean the state of arousal with which our bodies respond to demands made on them, a variation of what Walter B. Cannon described in the 1930s as the "fight or flight" response. This state of arousal includes the pounding heart, rapid breathing, dilated pupils, tensed muscles, and heightened alertness that enabled our ancestors to flee saber-toothed tigers and which today make us feel so rotten when we go to ask a saber-toothed tiger for a raise.

For our purposes, we do not really require an exact definition of stress; let's just say that stress is what we experience when our bodies and minds respond to any challenges or pressures presented to them. Stress is our reaction. In fact, we might look upon stress the way Supreme Court Justice Potter Stewart viewed pornography: it's hard to define, but we know it when we see it.

Keep in mind, though, that stress can be good. In many situations it's a good thing that our bodies and minds do respond; those responses *can* be very positive.

Here are some examples. When do athletes perform at

their peak? It's when the competition is the greatest, the pressure highest. We've all seen a division-leading baseball team play poorly against a last-place team and the next day play great ball against their second-place rivals. I've watched tennis champion Pete Sampras hit balls with his coach in practice. Sampras's shots were beautiful, but nothing like the awesome ones he hit later that day playing in a tournament final.

Ask a musician when he or she plays best: in the quiet of a rehearsal studio or on a stage in front of thousands of people? Why do film stars return to act on the stage? They often say that they *need* the "rush" they get performing before a live audience. That "rush" is their bodies' response to the challenge of performing live—that is stress.

For you, surgery is going to impose a stress on your body. And of course you want your body to respond. What's important, though, is that you perceive that response as a positive thing.

The Russian novelist Fyodor Dostoyevsky called psychology a sharp knife that cuts both ways. The same is true of stress. The way we respond to life's challenges—our stress—can work for us or against us. In fact, in different people the identical situation can evoke opposite stress responses. For instance, let's take a look at a tennis champion and me.

We both play tennis, but that's where the similarity ends. He wins almost all the time; I don't. When he goes out to play a big match, his pulse rate goes up as his heart sends additional blood to his tensing muscles to ready them for action. His digestion slows to divert blood to the muscles. Hormone messengers go out from his brain to prepare his liver to release more sugar and fat into the blood for energy. His breathing speeds up to provide more oxygen. He feels confident, in control, and raring to go.

When I play a big match, my heart also speeds up, but I sense it as a nervous pounding in my chest. My slowed digestion feels like butterflies in my stomach. My tense muscles make me hit my shots poorly. My fast breathing leaves me feeling short of breath. I feel lucky if I survive the first few games until I settle down. Two people, similar situations, similar body responses perceived very differently by both of them.

Fortunately, I don't play tennis for a living, and I'm a much better doctor than I am a tennis player. In my medical work, I love a challenge to my abilities. I really enjoy it when a colleague calls me in to consult on a patient with a difficult problem. I can almost feel my intellect become more keen; my senses sharpen as I prepare to examine the patient, alert to even the tiniest clues. No negative feelings here, even in a situation that can be extremely difficult.

We react to stress in ways that can benefit us or harm us. In fact, people are so different that even situations most of us would consider relaxing cause stress in some people. I have a patient named Carole who is a professional athlete. She is always active, constantly trying different sports and excelling at all of them. It seems to me she is always doing something new.

For a long time, Carole has had ulcerative colitis, a condition in which the large intestine becomes inflamed and irritated. No one knows exactly what causes ulcerative colitis, but many patients' symptoms worsen during times of stress. Carole's colitis has rarely kept her from her activities, though from time to time it would act up, and she would experience diarrhea with the passage of blood.

I heard from Carole a few months ago that she was pregnant, something she and her husband had been wanting for a long time. She was thrilled and happy, though she was often sick in the morning. I was concerned that her colitis would flare up, as it can in pregnancy, but it did not. As Carole's pregnancy progressed, she began to experience vaginal staining, so her obstetrician recommended that she stop participating in sports and take it easy. She spent time at home reading and watching TV.

Now, how many of us would love to be ordered to take it easy? Wouldn't it be nice to have someone tell us to take some time off and just relax at home? "Bob, your only responsibility is to hang out and take care of yourself." Sounds wonderful to me! But not to Carole.

After a few weeks at home she called me up to tell me that her colitis had flared up, giving her abdominal pain and diarrhea. I asked what happened, and she laughed and said, "I'm going nuts here." The laugh hid a lot of pain. For Carole, relaxing with nothing to do was far more stressful than the hectic life she enjoyed.

Whether events in your upcoming surgery put you under stress depends on how you react to it. Right now, your response is probably not something you can control. By the end of this chapter it will be. Or to paraphrase the Beatles on *Abbey Road:* In the end, the stress you take is equal to the stress you make.

STRESS AND CONTROL

What is it that differentiates good stress from bad? What makes the champion tennis player feel confident and me feel rotten? Why did Carole's colitis act up when she was forced to take it easy? One word: control.

A great tennis player has confidence in her shots, her knowledge of strategy; she feels in control of her game. The stress of competition works for her. I never know when my forehand will abandon me, when I will lose control. Stress works against me. Carole could not control her life and pursue the activities she enjoyed. Stress hurt her.

Let's take a closer look at the role of control in stress. Who do you think has the more stressful job, a worker on an automobile assembly line or the chief executive officer of the car company for which he works? The worker's job is repetitive, but would not seem particularly demanding. The executive has much more responsibility, since the lives of hundreds of people are affected by his actions. Furthermore, a poor decision on his part could cost his company millions of dollars.

On the surface, the answer seems pretty obvious. However, Dr. Robert Karasek and his research team from Columbia University learned that just the opposite is true. Assembly line workers feel more stress from their jobs than do the CEOs. The boring repetition combined with the constant pressure to perform at a certain level makes the workers' jobs psychologically demanding, but, unlike the executives, the workers have very little control over their jobs.

The executives can set their own hours, complete tasks in whatever order they wish, take breaks when they need them, eat in pleasant dining rooms, and stare out the windows of their fancy offices whenever they feel like it. The assembly line workers are stuck with performing set tasks at predetermined hours in a plant whose environment they can't influence. They may take a rest only when their union contract allows it, and there are probably no windows to stare out of.

The key here is control. An interesting Swedish study also demonstrated this. The researchers found that rail commuters who boarded at the beginning of a train's run found the journey less stressful than those who got on in the middle. This was true even though the early boarders' travel time was about twice that of the others. How could this be? It is probably because the early boarders were able to select their own seats, arrange their coats, and generally make themselves comfortable. In short, they could exert some control over their immediate environments. Those who got on later had to jostle for whatever seats were available or else stand, juggling their belongings; they had less control over their rides. Consequently, they found the commute more stressful.

Sometimes, just knowing you have some control reduces

the stress of a situation, even if you don't exercise that control. Drs. David C. Glass and Jerome E. Singer demonstrated this using noise to produce stress. These experimenters gave two groups of people various tasks to perform while being subjected to an objectionable noise. However, one group had a button they could push to silence the noise if it became too annoying. The second group had no means of eliminating the sound.

The first group generally finished their assigned tasks without pushing the silence button, so they were actually exposed to the same amount of noise as the group without access to the button. However, the group who could not eliminate the noise made more errors in their work, showed greater frustration, and even were less willing to help other people. Those who could have used the silence button showed almost no such behavior. The knowledge that they had some control reduced their stress.

The same thing applies to your surgery. As you will soon learn, there are many aspects of the surgical experience and your reaction to it that you can control. And just knowing that you have some control will reduce your stress. Right now, let's start to get some control over how you respond to stress.

A Simple Stress-Reducing Self-Relaxation/ Mental-Preparation Exercise

Over the centuries people have developed many techniques for reducing stress. There are countless forms of meditation, as varied as the cultures that developed them, as well as self-hypnosis, visualization, and the relaxation response. If you have the time and interest, you might want to consult some of the books in the Annotated Bibliography regarding these methods. Some techniques are easy to learn, while others require extensive training and practice.

What I have done here is taken some of the best techniques and combined them into a simple, easily mastered exercise. It's so simple, in fact, that while you're doing it, you may feel that nothing is happening. For the moment, take my word for it that something *is* happening in your brain. Afterward, when you see how good you feel, you'll know I was right.

This exercise serves several purposes to help you through surgery. First, you are going to reduce stress and thereby start to feel better in general and about your upcoming surgery in particular. Second, you will be starting to train yourself in active mind-body cooperation. As you saw with the imaginary lemon exercise in Chapter 1, the mind-body connection is already in place. By practicing the following exercise, you will be starting to learn how to take conscious advantage of it. Finally, this exercise is the foundation on which all the others in this book are based. Mastering self-relaxation will enable you to learn to limit blood loss, reduce pain, and accelerate recovery.

First I'll describe the technique to you so that you'll understand what you're doing. *Don't try it yet; just read the description.* Right afterward I'll give you the instructions in the form of a script that someone can read aloud to you or, better, that you can read yourself into a tape recorder. That way, you can practice the technique without worrying that you'll make a mistake or leave something out. (Also available is a professionally recorded tape of my own mellifluous voice reading the script and taking you through the self-relaxation. See the page at the back of the book for ordering information.)

The relaxation exercise has five parts. First, we'll do some controlled breathing. Then we will relax every muscle in your body, starting from the top of your head and working slowly downward to the tips of your toes. Next come some techniques to produce a deep state of mental calm, followed by some visualization techniques to release stress. Finally, we will return to your usual state of mental functioning.

Reading the script at a calm, slow pace, the exercise takes about twenty-two minutes. The first several times you do this I recommend using this long version, the training-wheel script, if you will. However, the technique is so easy to learn that you will very soon find that your mind is racing ahead of the tape, and that it is holding you back. Therefore, I've given you a condensed nine-minute version to practice with regularly. As you practice (more about practicing later), you may even find that you can do self-relaxation without the tape. That's fine now and again—say, if you want to practice and you don't have your tape with you. For the most part, though, I suggest you practice with the tape, because the specific suggestions in its script are important for improving your surgical outcome.

The technique you are about to learn is one hundred percent safe. There is no possibility of physical or mental harm. It is not a trance or a loss of self-control or a giving up of your will to another person. What you are really doing is learning to bring out a natural mental state that up till now you have never learned to control. Your mind will be alert and fully functioning, and yet you will feel remarkably calm and relaxed.

Here is a pretty good analogy to what you are going to experience. Imagine you are sitting in a crowded room reading an absolutely fascinating book. The book is so absorbing that at times you are barely aware of the people around you. Sometimes your thoughts wander, though, and you might "tune in" to a conversation going on nearby. Soon, however, the book draws you back, and you lose yourself in it once again.

Here, instead of directing your attention to a book, you will be directing your attention inward into yourself. At times, your thoughts may wander. That's okay. Just let those thoughts play themselves out, and then return to your self-relaxation exercise.

The most important thing to keep in mind is not to try too hard. No need to think to yourself, "C'mon, relax, dammit. Let's go! Relax! Relax!" All you have to do is go through the motions, and your mind will take over. *Don't make anything happen; simply let it happen*.

THE SETTING

This self-relaxation/mental-preparation exercise is best done in a fairly quiet place where you will be left alone. The quiet is not so important as the solitude. If you are at home, tell everyone else that you need to practice your self-relaxation, go into a room by yourself, and close the door. Tell someone else to answer the phone or take it off the hook. (Don't start practicing until the phone stops making that horrible "off-the-hook" noise. It takes about a minute and a half from when you first take the phone off.)

There are plenty of other places where you can practice your mental exercises. If you commute to work, a train or subway is fine. (Not behind the wheel of a car, please.) Practicing in an office or other workplace is a bit trickier since anyone who sees you will think you are sleeping on the job. If you have a private office, you can close the door and activate your voice mail. ("I'm not in my usual state of consciousness right now. Please leave a message . . .") Several of my patients practice at work in a closed bathroom stall. No one bothers them in there!

You can do your self-relaxation indoors or out-of-doors. I once tried to do it in New York's Central Park, but I was unsuccessful since I kept opening my eyes to make sure that no one was sneaking up to mug me. So pick a safe, secure place.

If you are practicing at home, sit upright in a comfortable chair. A recliner is okay, but don't do this in bed. The idea is not to fall asleep, something easy to do when you are relaxing so deeply.

THE TECHNIQUE

Here is a description of what you are going to be doing. Again, *don't do it yet*. The actual instructions follow in the form of a script.

Sit upright in your chair with the back of the chair supporting the small of your back. Your legs should be uncrossed, with your feet resting flat on the floor. Place your hands either comfortably in your lap or on the armrests of the chair.

Look above your line of sight and pick out a spot high up on the opposite wall to look at. This could be a point of interest in a picture, a word on the spine of a book on a shelf, or just an irregularity in the wall itself. The idea is to fix your attention on this spot and continue to do so until you close your eyes in a few moments.

As you direct your attention to the spot opposite you, you become aware of your breathing. Normally, we are not conscious of our breathing from moment to moment, so when starting a self-relaxation, simply become aware of the fact that you are breathing in and breathing out. You don't have to breathe in a particular way, just be aware that it is happening.

Next take three slow, deep breaths in through your nose and then let them out slowly through your mouth. This is very controlled, easy breathing. Do not hold your breath at the end of each inhalation. Simply take the breath in slowly and let it out even more slowly. Repeat this three times.

On the third breath, as you exhale slowly, simply allow your eyes to close gently. Then forget about your spot on the wall, forget about your breathing, and start the process of relaxation.

The technique of muscle relaxation is called progressive relaxation. There are a number of ways to do it; I think this is the simplest. What you do is simply become aware of certain groups of muscles and then consciously relax them. In other words, first feel the muscles *with your mind*. Just become aware of their presence. Then relax the muscles. You might want to imagine that the muscles are turning to rubber and growing limp. Or that they are getting very heavy and leaden. One technique that works well is to imagine that the muscles are filling up with warm, heavy molasses. If this concept of willing muscles to relax seems difficult to you, simply follow the instructions as they are given in the script, and it will come to you quite easily.

Certain groups of muscles may feel particularly tight, for instance those of the back of your neck and upper back. Do not try to force the muscles to relax. Simply ease the tightness out of them. There is no rush. If a particular group of muscles takes a bit longer to relax, no problem. You're not rushing off anywhere.

Some people like to think relaxing words to themselves along with the tape. For instance, "I am becoming aware of the muscles on top of my head. There is tightness and tension there. Now I am allowing those muscles to relax. I feel the tension and tightness going out of the muscles, and they are becoming heavy, limp, and relaxed. Now I can feel the muscles of my forehead . . ." Many people start off thinking these words but soon find that they simply feel the relaxation without having to think the words.

The order of the muscle groups is as follows:

Top of the head
Forehead, eyebrows, and eyelids
Cheeks and jaw; let the lips separate a little
Front of the neck
Back of the neck
Across the top of the shoulders
Upper back muscles
Lower back muscles
Chest
Abdomen and waist
Upper arms
Forearms
Wrists, hands, and fingers
Hips

Thighs and upper legs
Calves
Ankles, feet, and toes

After you have done this relaxation, you may notice a strange sensation of separation between your body and your mind. Your body will feel relaxed, but your mind will be very alert. Next come some techniques to deepen the state of mental relaxation.

There are actually several ways to do this. Choose one that seems appealing to you. Some people like to count backward *very slowly* from ten to one along with the tape. Another technique that works well is to imagine a deep, still pool and think of your mind as becoming as still as that pool. Some people like to deepen their mental state by visualizing pictures in their minds. They see themselves riding an elevator down to the lowest floor of a building or taking a very long escalator ride down to the bottom. Another technique is to imagine yourself sinking in slow motion into the deepest, most comfortable armchair that you can imagine. Choose whatever deepening technique works best for you. The script combines several.

YOUR "SPECIAL PLACE"

Once you are complete relaxed, you are going to take an imaginary journey to the most peaceful, relaxing, secure, stress-free place you can imagine. We will refer to this throughout the book as your "special place."

This can be any place you want it to be. Perhaps it is somewhere you once went on vacation where you felt completely relaxed. Perhaps it is some place from your childhood. (For instance, one of my patients likes to imagine he is sitting in a rocking chair in his grandmother's house.) Perhaps your special place is a peaceful activity such as fishing or sailing.

Your special place does not even have to be real. It might

only exist in your imagination. A perfect Caribbean beach that you have all to yourself. A mountaintop meadow where you can see for miles (remember Julie Andrews at the beginning of *The Sound of Music?*). A walk through a cool woods with a little babbling brook. Sunning yourself on the deck of your personal 150-foot yacht.

Whatever place you choose, it must have two important characteristics. Above all, it must be the most calming, secure, stress-free place *you* can imagine. The choice of place must come from within you.

Second, your place should have characteristics that you can perceive with several of your senses. You should be able to *see* the place in your mind's eye. Make the colors vibrant. If there is open sky, it is the deepest and richest blue you can imagine. Same thing for water. If there is foliage, it is a lush green. Clouds are a brilliant white. See the details of your special place right down to individual blades of grass or grains of sand.

Your special place should have sounds that you can *hear* in your imagination: gentle waves lapping against the shore, a wind blowing softly through nearby trees, the voices of children playing in the distance, even the rumble of traffic far away.

Even the senses of *touch* and *smell* come into play. You should be aware of the feelings of your special place. Perhaps it is the sun warming you, or a breeze blowing gently through your hair. Even try to smell the scents of your place—the fresh salty ocean air, the flowers in a meadow, the pie your grandmother just baked, etc. Don't forget about *taste*. Maybe you are sipping a cool drink on that beach.

Whatever special place you choose, try to use all the senses of your imagination to experience actually being there. See your place. Hear it, feel it, smell it, and even taste it. Make it as real and totally involving of all the senses as you can. Be there. As you do, you will feel all stress and tension slipping right out of you. An extraordinary sensation of calm will come over you. You will feel deeply at peace.

BACK TO REALITY

You end the practice session by counting slowly from *one* to *ten*. With each count, you'll feel yourself lightening up, feel energy returning to your arms and legs. When you reach *eight*, take a deep cleansing breath and then let all the air out. After you count *ten*, open your eyes when you feel ready.

Don't jump up right away. You are going to feel mellow, calm, and at peace. Let the feeling last. You will be surprised, though, that when you return to your usual activities, a sensation of calm will remain with you.

Here is a review of the steps of this self-relaxation exercise:

1. Find a place where you can be left alone.
2. Sit upright in a comfortable chair.
3. Select a spot high up on the opposite wall.
4. Become aware of your breathing.
5. Take three slow, deep breaths in and release slowly.
6. On the third breath close your eyes.
7. Progressively relax your muscles from head to toes.
8. Deepen your relaxation by counting backward or riding the escalator, etc.
9. Visit your special place; use all of your senses.
10. Return to your usual state of mind by counting from *one* to *ten*.

Don't worry if your mind wanders as you perform this exercise. Also, don't be concerned if troubling thoughts come to mind. Simply let these thoughts—worrisome or otherwise—float away. Some experts in meditation, such as Harvard's Dr. Herbert Benson, suggest simply thinking, "Oh, well . . ." when such thoughts intrude, letting the thoughts slip away, and then returning to what you were doing. Teachers of Transcendental Meditation suggest thinking of such thoughts as tiny air bubbles floating to the surface of a swimming pool.

The bubbles (thoughts) float lazily upward, and when they reach the surface, *POP!* they just disappear.

Just let extraneous thoughts go. Don't force them out of your mind. Let them go on their way and then gently bring yourself back to your mental exercise.

Practice Makes You-Know-What

The self-relaxation/mental-preparation technique described above serves as the basis for almost all the mind-body techniques we are going to employ to help you through surgery, so it is crucial that you practice it.

Don't worry if not much seems to happen the first time you try it. It doesn't matter if you feel as if you're just going through the motions. Things are starting to happen inside. Your mind is learning to achieve a new state of consciousness. It's not going to happen immediately.

Remember the first time you tried to ride a bicycle? Did you just jump on, start pedaling, and go? I doubt it. You had to learn to find your balance, to coordinate your hands and feet, to start and stop. But with practice, riding a bicycle became second nature. Your mind learned how to tell your body what to do. And now you could get on a bike and ride easily no matter how long it's been since you last did it. Your mind and body learned.

Sometimes my patients ask me how I know that they will be able to learn this technique as well as they need to for surgery. I tell them that learning self-relaxation is like learning to play the piano. If you have great inborn talent, you might one day become a great concert pianist. But even if you have no talent whatsoever, you can still learn to play a pretty tune. To help yourself through surgery, all you have to learn is the pretty tune.

And learning comes with practice. To continue the piano analogy, you can go to the greatest teacher in the world, but if you don't practice, you'll never learn to play the piano. I could give you the best self-relaxation technique around (and I have!), but without practice, you'll never learn to do it.

We're not talking about a large time commitment here, so I don't want to hear about your being too busy to practice. Heck, if you listen to the tape for twenty minutes twice a day, that's less than one out of twenty-four hours in the day. Very soon you'll change over to the short version of the tape, and you'll be able to do a self-relaxation in nine minutes, three times a day. That's twenty-seven out of 1,440 minutes in a day. Less than two percent of each day. You can't find time for that?

Remember, you're going to feel great every time you do a self-relaxation. You'll also experience much less stress in your daily life because you will be releasing stressful feelings regularly. And don't forget why we're here. The goal is to improve your surgical outcome through mind-body training. With this exercise you will be starting to learn to control the mind-body connection. So practice. PRACTICE. *PRACTICE*. You're doing this for you.

Self-Relaxation/Mental Preparation Script

It's hard to learn a new technique just from reading instructions. (Imagine trying to learn to ride a bicycle by reading a booklet on the subject.) Just closing your eyes and letting someone lead you through the steps of self-relaxation will be immensely easier. I can do it for you on the available tape. Or you can do it for yourself by reading the following script into a tape recorder and then playing the tape back for yourself. It's best to listen through headphones, if you have them. If you do not have access to a tape recorder, have someone else read the script for you.

Some things to remember as you make your tape or as someone reads to you:

• Read slowly and clearly in a calm, soothing voice.

- Where I put in a dotted line (. . .), pause for a few seconds.

- Where I have put [*Your Name*], insert your first name. Yes, say your own name to yourself. You are giving yourself instructions.

- Instructions to be followed by the reader but not to be actually read aloud are [**boldface in brackets**].

- When you get to the description of your "special place," feel free to modify my words to fit your particular place. Just make sure that your description details all the things you will see, hear, feel, smell, and taste.

- Otherwise, please read the script *exactly as written*. Even though it may seem dull and repetitive as you read it aloud, every instruction is there for a reason. Please don't leave anything out.

At first, you will want to use this tape every time you practice self-relaxation. Pretty soon, though, you will find that you no longer need the detailed instructions in the script. Your own relaxation will be speeding along ahead of the tape. At that point, change to the shorter version that follows.

Don't discard your original tape, though. You may find after a while that you feel as if you are losing the ability to relax as deeply as you had been. That's the time to listen to the extended version again to reinforce your abilities.

◆

Okay, [*Your Name*], sit comfortably in your chair with the back of the chair supporting your back and your feet flat on the floor. . . . As you sit comfortably and relaxed, pick out a spot on the opposite wall well above your eye level and look right at that spot. Just direct all your attention to that spot opposite you as you listen to me, casually and effortlessly. Just keep looking there. Good.

Now, as you continue to concentrate on that spot on the wall, I want you to become aware of your breathing. Just become aware of the fact that you are breathing and feel the air flowing in and flowing out. You don't have to breathe deeply or in any special way. Simply feel the air flow in . . . and flow out. That's good. You are continuing to look at the spot opposite you, but you are aware of the air flowing in . . . and flowing out.

You are going to find that as you breathe, each time you exhale, each time you breathe out, you are going to feel a bit more relaxed. That is, you will note that each time you exhale, your body will feel a bit heavier and a bit more relaxed than it did a moment before. You continue to look at your spot, but notice how a pleasant sense of heaviness is just starting to set in. **[Pause a few seconds to let this feeling happen.]**

That's good. Now on to the next breath, take a deep breath in through your nose and let it out slowly through your mouth. . . . That's good. Deep breath in, and let it out slowly through your mouth. **[Allow a few seconds for a deep, slow breath.]** Fine. And once again, a deep slow breath in through your nose, and let it out slowly through your mouth. **[Another few seconds.]** Good. Now, on the next deep breath as you let the breath out slowly, just let your eyes drift closed. **[Few-second pause.]** Just forget about your breathing, forget about the spot you were looking at. Simply relax with your eyes closed and listen to me.

What we are going to do now is relax your body from the top of your head to the tips of your toes. The way we are going to do that is by becoming aware of different groups of muscles, relaxing them, and then forgetting about them. So right now, please become aware of the muscles on top of your head. Simply be aware of their presence. Feel them with your mind. . . .

And now, let those muscles relax. There are several ways to do this. Some people like to imagine that the muscles are getting heavy and limp. Others, that the muscles are getting rubbery and loose. Still other people like to imagine that the muscles are filling up with warm, pleasant molasses. Whatever you want to do is fine. Just feel the muscles on top of your head starting to relax. Feel the tightness flow out of them. Don't force the muscles to relax, simply *allow* them to relax. . . . That's fine. The muscles on top of your head become heavy, pleasant, and relaxed.

Now let's forget about those muscles and go down to the muscles of your forehead, and around your eyebrows and eyelids.

Feel those muscles with your mind. . . . Become conscious of them. . . . Now let them relax. If you are crinkling your brow, uncrinkle it. Almost feel the wrinkles in your forehead smoothing out as the muscles there relax. Your eyelids are relaxed. They feel heavy, as if it would be an effort to open them. But you don't even want to be bothered opening them. All you want to do is let the muscles of your forehead, eyebrows, and eyelids become relaxed.

Very good. Now to the muscles of your face and cheeks and jaw. If your jaw is clenched, unclench it. Let your lips part a little. Almost imagine that you can feel the muscles of your face hanging, sagging, drooping on the bones of your face. . . . All the muscles of your face become deeply, pleasantly relaxed.

You're doing very well. This is easy, so let's go on to the muscles of your neck. Feel the neck muscles, both front and back. Be aware that we often store a lot of tension in those neck muscles. Feel if there is tightness there. Now let that tightness go. . . . Just ease it right out of those muscles. Feel the neck muscles become limp and relaxed.

Now to the muscles across the tops of your shoulders. Feel the muscles there, . . . ease the tension and tightness right out of them, . . . and let those muscles relax. As you do so, you might notice that your shoulders sag a bit. Your arms feel a bit heavier at your sides. Because the muscles of your shoulders are becoming heavy, limp, and relaxed.

Now let's go to the muscles across your upper back, across your shoulder blades. As we go down your body, you may want to think the words along with me. In other words, you might want to think to yourself, "I can feel the muscles of my upper back. I am aware of tension and tightness there. Now I am letting that tension and tightness go. The muscles of my upper back are relaxing." Or you may simply prefer to feel the relaxation happen without thinking any words to yourself. Whichever you prefer is fine. Just ease the tension and tightness out of the muscles of your upper back, and let those muscles relax.

You may find, as the muscles of your neck, shoulders, and upper back relax, that your head wants to nod forward, or it may want to tip to one side, or it may want to stay exactly where it is. Whatever your head wants to do is fine. Just let it happen.

As we go down through your body, you might notice certain other things. For instance, you might notice a change in the pattern of your breathing. Your breathing might become slow and regular. Or you might feel a tingling in your hands, arms, or feet. Not everyone experiences these things, but if you do, just be aware that these are part of the relaxation process and don't be concerned about them.

From your upper back, let's move down to your lower back. Feel the muscles of your lower back. Feel the chair pressing up against them. Now let those muscles grow limp and relaxed . . . deeply, pleasantly relaxed.

Okay, let's proceed now to the muscles of your chest. Feel the muscles with your mind, relax them, and forget about them. . . . Again, as your chest muscles relax, you may notice a change in the pattern of your breathing. That's fine. Just let it happen.

From the chest down to the muscles around your waist. You're getting good at this now. Just let those muscles relax and forget about them.

Now to the muscles of your arms. First feel the muscles of your upper arms, both front and back. Biceps and triceps. Good. Now let those muscles grow limp and relaxed. Let your arms grow heavy at your sides. . . . Now let this warm, pleasant feeling of heaviness go down past your elbows into your forearms. . . . And through your wrists. . . . Into your hands and all the way down to the tips of your fingers, so that now the muscles of your arms are so heavy, limp, and relaxed that your arms feel like two great lead weights that you couldn't lift even if you wanted to. But you don't even want to. All you want to do is go deeply, pleasantly relaxed.

Now, [Your Name], please notice, as you relax deeply and well, that you are aware of everything that is going on. You hear my voice. You are fully in control. You are simply allowing these things to happen. It feels good to relax deeply and well, and you would like to relax even more. So let's keep going.

Become aware of the muscles of your buttocks and hips. Feel the muscles . . . relax them . . . and forget about them.

Now down to the muscles of your thighs and upper legs. Those muscles become very heavy . . . very limp . . . and very relaxed. The heaviness and relaxation are spreading right down through you.

Okay, feel your calf muscles now. And let them relax. . . . And let the feeling of heavy relaxation spread down past your ankles, into your feet, and all the way down to the tips of your toes. So that now your legs feel like two great lead weights that you couldn't lift even if you wanted to. But, again, you don't even want to.

That's very good, [Your Name]. You've done very well. Notice that you feel relaxed and calm and completely in control. You feel very relaxed and very good, and it would be very nice to relax even more deeply. To help you do that, I'm going to count backward very slowly from ten to one. As I do, with each count, you'll feel yourself becoming more deeply relaxed. More deeply relaxed with each count, so that by the time I reach one, you will be in the deepest possible state of relaxation—completely free from stress, strain, and tension.

Here we go, now. *Ten*. It's going to be very nice to relax so deeply and so well. **[Three-to-five-second pause before saying each number.]** . . . *Nine*. It's a nice pleasant feeling, so just let it happen. . . . *Eight*. You are allowing yourself to go ever more deeply relaxed. You might want to imagine that you are riding a long escalator or elevator down to the deepest possible state of relaxation. . . . *Seven*. Your mind becomes like a deep, still pool. A wonderful feeling of peace and calm is coming over you. Any extraneous thoughts just slip away. . . . *Six*. Imagine a beautiful mountain lake at dawn. It is perfectly still. There is not even the slightest breeze. No animals are stirring. The surface of the lake is like a perfect silver mirror. That's the complete feeling of calm that is coming over you. . . .

Five. It's wonderful to relax so deeply, and yet you would like to relax even more. . . . *Four*. Free of stress. Free of strain. Wonderfully, pleasantly relaxed. . . . *Three*. You've never been this deeply relaxed before. Your mind is deep and still. Any extraneous thoughts just drift away. And you would like to go deeper still. . . . *Two*. Approaching the deepest possible state of relaxation. . . . And *One*. Completely, totally relaxed.

That's great, [Your Name]. Notice the deep, pleasant feeling of calm you have. You are completely in control, but you have allowed yourself to relax so very deeply.

As you relax deeply and well, let's take a journey to the most beautiful, peaceful, relaxing place on earth you can possibly imagine. Your special place. And we're going to use all the senses of your imagination to experience actually being there. So right now, in your mind's eye, see yourself in your special place. Actually see this place in your mind. See it in great detail. Depending on where you are, see the individual grains of sand. Or single blades of grass. Or each leaf on each tree. See how beautiful it is. The colors are the most vibrant you can imagine. The sky is a beautiful, rich blue. If there is water, it is the deepest blue you have ever seen. Plants are a lush green. You can see every detail of your special place in your mind. . . .

Hear the sounds of your special place. Maybe it's the sound of waves coming gently on shore. Or a soft breeze blowing through some nearby trees. Or the familiar sounds of an old house. Or some children playing in the distance. Just hear the sounds of your beautiful, special place. . . .

Feel the feelings of your special place. Perhaps you are basking in a warm, gentle sun. Maybe there is a soft breeze blowing through your hair. If there is sand, let it run over your fingers. It feels so good to be here. Just enjoy the feelings. . . .

Even smell the scents of this beautiful, special place. The fresh ocean air. Or maybe the smell of a cool meadow. Or a deep woods. Whatever it may be, enjoy the smells of your special place. . . . If there are any tastes associated with your place, even enjoy them, too.

Experience the wonderful, relaxing calm of being in your special place. See it. Hear it. Feel it. Smell it. It's so wonderful to be here. Notice how all anxiety, stress, and strain just melt away. You feel so very relaxed, so calm. So good. Nothing is bothering you at the moment, and it's wonderful to feel so very good. . . . Just enjoy this marvelous, peaceful calm.

And [Your Name], the best part is that this feeling of complete and total calm will stay with you even when you have completed your relaxation practice. In a few minutes, when you return to everyday life, you will notice a wonderful sense of peace. You'll feel calm and relaxed. You'll enjoy the rest of the day, and things that were bothering you before will barely disturb you at all. You have released all tension, stress, and strain, so that when you return to your usual state of mind, you will feel wonderfully peaceful, relaxed, and calm.

You'll find that you will handle any situation that comes up with ease and grace. You'll be relaxed and refreshed, and your mind will function clearly and well, as if all the cobwebs had been cleared away. You will feel just great for the rest of the day.

And you'll notice that as you continue to practice these self-relaxation exercises, you will feel better and better in everyday life. Your concerns about your upcoming surgery will lessen, and you'll realize that you are gaining a degree of control over your mind and body that will greatly help you through surgery. Stress, strain, and anxiety will become less and less a part of your life with every passing day. And you will feel relaxed and calm and good. Through the immense power of your mind, you are getting control of the situation, and you are going to have an excellent outcome.

Now, [Your Name], once again visit your special place. See it. Hear it. Feel it. Sense it in every way. . . . Enjoy being there. And notice how very good you feel. . . .

In a couple of minutes, we are going to return you to your usual state of consciousness. When we do, you will feel marvelously relaxed and calm, yet fully alert and fully awake. You are going to feel just great. The way we'll do this is simply by counting from one to ten. When I reach ten, you will open your eyes and feel marvelously refreshed and relaxed, having enjoyed this practice session immensely and looking forward to continuing to use these exercises for your own benefit.

Okay. Here we go. One. . . . Two. Feel yourself starting to lighten up just a bit. . . . Three. . . . Four. Energy is starting to return to your arms and legs. . . . Five. . . . Six. You might want to wiggle your fingers and toes to get the blood circulating again. . . . Seven. Feeling very good now. . . . Eight. Take a deep, cleansing breath . . . and let it all the way out. . . . Nine. Just about ready to open your eyes. . . . And Ten, whenever you feel ready, you may open your eyes and feel relaxed and calm and just great.

Now just sit and relax for a few minutes and enjoy this good feeling. Then, when you feel ready, you may turn off the tape.

That's it! The first time you listen to your tape or have the script read to you, you may wonder if anything happened. After all, you were alert and awake the whole time. You didn't go into a trance and come back, not knowing where you had been. You may even have felt at times that you were observing what was going on and not really experiencing much.

If you believe that nothing happened, that you did not achieve a different state of mind, let me ask you this: Can you think of any other circumstance in which you could sit in a chair for twenty-two minutes without moving a muscle? Without wiggling around or scratching or getting up to go to the bathroom? After you sit in a chair and watch TV for twenty-two minutes, do you feel as mellow and calm as you did after you listened to the tape? The answer to these questions is most certainly no.

Things did start happening in your mind, but on an *unconscious* level. Therefore, you could not be *consciously* aware of them. All you could perceive after your first experience was the wonderful feeling you had afterward. However, as you practice, you will start to notice several things:

- You will very quickly get the hang of how to perform a self-relaxation and will be able to do it much faster than the description on the tape. That's when to switch to the shorter version that follows.

- Your anxiety about your upcoming surgery will lessen. You will realize that you are starting to get control of your feelings and of body processes.

- You will experience less stress in your life. This beneficial effect sort of sneaks up on you. It's not that after performing the exercises a few times you will say to yourself, "Wow! I'm a new person. Nothing bothers me anymore." Rather, you'll notice that people and things that formerly would cause you to feel stress simply do so less and less.

• You will start to think of other things you can use these mental exercises for. If you have a headache, for instance, as you visit your special place you can tell yourself that when the practice session is over, the tension and tightness in your head will be relieved and your headache will be gone. If you are having difficulty sleeping at night, tell yourself during your practice sessions that you will fall asleep quickly and deeply that night. Just repeat to yourself a few times any suggestions for what you want to achieve. Your conscious mind will be talking to your unconscious mind. You'll be surprised at how effective this technique is.

As I said above, these things will not occur right at the outset. You will have to practice the self-relaxation regularly. But as with so many things in life, the first time is not necessarily the best time. The more you do it, the better you'll get at it and the more you'll enjoy it.

Self-Relaxation Script—the Short Version

As I mentioned earlier, you will learn very quickly how to do your mental-preparation/self-relaxation exercises. Then the script above will seem excruciatingly long to sit through. You will find your mind racing ahead of the tape.

Therefore, I have included a script for a nine-minute self-relaxation below. It takes you through the same steps as the long version, but the instructions are less detailed. (I have also included this version on the separately available tape that I have prepared for you.)

This exercise spends less time on getting you relaxed and more time on the mind-body preparation needed for surgery. Once you have mastered the techniques of self-relaxation using the long version, switch to this one. How will you know when you're ready to make the switch? You'll know.

◆

Okay, [*Your Name*], sit comfortably in your chair with your feet flat on the floor and listen to me. First, pick out a spot high up on the opposite wall and fix your attention on that spot. Just listen to my voice casually and effortlessly. . . . As you look at the spot, become aware of your breathing. Simply feel the air flowing in and flowing out. . . . Flowing in and flowing out. That's fine. . . .

On the next breath, take a deep breath in through your nose and let it out slowly through your mouth. **[Pause enough time to do this.]** And once again. Deep breath in . . . and let it out slowly through your mouth. . . . And now a deep breath in and hold it. And as you let your breath out slowly, let your eyes drift closed. . . . Now just forget about your breathing, forget about your eyes, and let's relax you top to bottom.

[Read the next five paragraphs at a rate that matches how quickly you want to do the progressive muscle relaxation.]

Starting at the top of your head, feel the muscles up there, and let them relax. Just become aware of those muscles, and allow them to become very heavy, very limp, and very relaxed. . . . Now down to the muscles of your forehead, and eyebrows, and eyelids. Just feel those muscles and let them go. Imagine that the wrinkles of your brow are smoothing out and that the eyelids are growing heavy and limp. . . .

Now let the muscles of your face relax . . . Your lips part a little, and your jaw becomes limp. Let the muscles in your head and face become deeply, pleasantly relaxed. . . .

Let's go now to the muscles of your neck. Feel the tightness there, and let it go. . . . Now to your shoulders, across the tops of your shoulders. Feel them become heavy and limp, and feel your arms droop a bit more by your sides. . . . Become aware now of the muscles across your upper back, and let them relax. . . . And to the lower back. All the muscles of your back become heavy, limp, and relaxed.

Chest muscles now. Feel them, relax them, and forget about them. . . . And down to the muscles around your waist. Feel those muscles and let them go. . . . Upper arms, both front and back. Become aware of the muscles of the upper arms and let them relax. . . . And let this warm, pleasant feeling of heaviness extend down into your forearms. And your wrists, and hands, and right down to the tips of your fingers. So that your arm muscles are so heavy and limp and relaxed that your arms feel like two great lead weights, so heavy that you couldn't lift them even if you wanted to. But you don't even want to.

That's fine, [Your Name], you're doing very well, and the whole upper half of your body feels heavy, limp, and relaxed. So let's go to the lower half. Feel the muscles of your buttocks and hips and let them go. . . .

And let this feeling of heaviness spread down into your thighs and upper legs. . . . Past your knees into your calves. . . . And all the way down your ankles and feet to the tips of your toes. So that now the leg muscles feel so heavy, limp, and relaxed that your legs feel like two great lead weights that you couldn't lift even if you wanted to. But, again, you don't even want to.

Very, very good, [Your Name]. You are relaxing deeply and well, and it would be so nice to relax even more deeply. So let's do that now. I'm going to count backward from ten to one. As I do so, with each count you will become many times more deeply relaxed. Stress, tension, and anxiety will flow out of you, and you will feel very, very good.

[During the counting, use whatever mental images help you to relax more deeply—an elevator, escalator, deep easy chair, mountain lake, etc.]

Here we go. *Ten*. Deeply, pleasantly relaxed. . . . *Nine*. It's a nice, pleasant sinking feeling. So just let it happen. . . . *Eight*. Every time I mention deeper relaxation, you go many times more deeply relaxed. . . . *Seven*. Your mind becomes like a deep, still pool. . . . *Six*. All extraneous thoughts just sort of drift away. . . . *Five*. Going ever more deeply relaxed. . . . *Four*. All stress, tension, and anxiety just flow out of you. . . . *Three.* You've never been this deeply relaxed before. And yet you would like to go deeper still. . . . *Two.* Ready for the deepest possible relaxation. . . . And *One.* Deeply, pleasantly relaxed.

[Fill in the blanks in the paragraph with descriptions of your own "special place."]

Very good, [*Your Name*]. Now let's take a journey to your special place. And remember to use all the senses of your imagination to experience actually being there. So now, see this beautiful, special place in your mind. See all the details of [_____], all the beautiful colors. . . . Hear the sounds of your special place. Hear the [_____]. . . . Feel the feelings of this wonderful place. Feel [_____]. . . . Even smell the scents of this place, the [_____]. Use every sense of your imagination to experience being there.

And as you do, notice how good you feel. Free of stress. Free of tension. Free of anxiety. . . . You feel calm, peaceful, and good. You have a very positive feeling about your upcoming surgery. You know that you are gaining control over your mind and your body. And you will be able to use this control to greatly improve your outcome from surgery. You are going to have a very successful, very comfortable surgical experience. You are going to recover quickly and completely. You will feel very positive about your upcoming surgery, and you will have a feeling of peaceful calm about the whole surgical experience.

Now once again visit your special place. See it. And hear it. Feel it and smell it. Even taste it. And notice how very good and very peaceful you feel. . . .

Now, [*Your Name*], in a few moments I am going to help you to return to your usual state of consciousness. When you open your eyes, you will feel completely calm and completely relaxed. And yet you will feel full of vibrant energy, ready to go about the tasks of the day feeling very calm, yet very energized and very good.

[Pace the next paragraph to match the rate at which you like to return to normal consciousness.]

When I count to five, you will open your eyes and feel very good. *One*. Starting to return to your normal state of mind. . . . *Two*. Feel yourself lightening up. Feel energy starting to return to your arms and legs. . . . *Three*. Wiggle your fingers and toes a little to get the circulation going again. . . . *Four*. Take a deep, cleansing breath, and let it all the way out. . . . And whenever you feel ready, *Five*, you may open your eyes and feel absolutely great.

As you have noticed, this script gives very general preparation for your surgery. It is intended to relieve stress and to strengthen your mind-body connection. Starting about three or four days before your surgery, you will change over to the very specific mind-body preparation designed for upcoming surgery. You will find the presurgical script in Part II.

If your operation *is* in the next few days, use the long tape several times today. Then use the short script once or twice before switching over to the presurgical script.

Sometimes patients ask me, "Can you do these exercises too much?" The answer is no, not really. You cannot harm yourself with them, but if you do them to excess, you will become bored with them and they will lose their effectiveness. Certainly practice until you feel comfortable doing the exercises, but not to the point that they become routine.

Now you are starting to take control of the surgical experience. You are preparing your mind and your body. You are preparing to be an active participant in your surgery, mustering all your natural forces to help yourself through. While you do this, it is important to know in great detail exactly what you are going to experience. So while you are relieving stress and preparing your mind, read on to gain more knowledge and thereby more power.

CHAPTER CHECKLIST

☐ Prepare a "long version" self-relaxation tape.

☐ Practice the long version twice a day for a few days by listening to your tape, having someone read the script to you, or listening to my tape.

☐ When the long version starts to feel too long, prepare a tape of the condensed exercise and listen to it three times daily.

☐ Three or four days before surgery prepare a tape using the presurgical script and practice three times daily (see Part II).

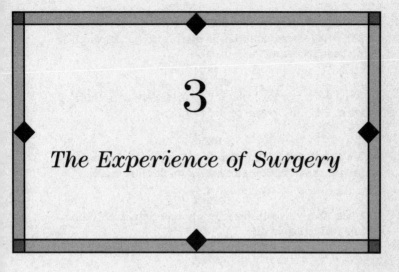

3

The Experience of Surgery

Imagine this scene from some future secret-agent movie:

OFFICE OF MR. GREEN, HEAD OF THE COMPANY.

AGENT BROWN is summoned into MR. GREEN's office. He leaves MISS SMITH's outer office, where he has been flirting with the comely secretary.

> GREEN
> Come in, Brown. Please take a seat.

> BROWN
> Thank you, sir.

> GREEN
> I have just completed a meeting with the President. We are sending you on a most extraordinary secret operation.

> BROWN
> May I inquire as to the nature of the operation?

GREEN

I'm afraid not. Your job is simply to get through it as best you can.

BROWN

I beg your pardon, sir. But I must have some idea of what I am supposed to accomplish.

GREEN

Let's just say that it is a "surgical strike" against a target that the Company feels must be removed.

BROWN

I see. Can you tell me who my contacts are? Whom am I to work with?

GREEN

I'm afraid that's classified.

BROWN

Well, there must be certain procedures to be followed. What are the rules of engagement?

GREEN

I'm not allowed to say.

BROWN

Dammit, Green! You are sending me to perform some type of surgical operation with no information. How can you expect me to succeed? I hope at least that I'll be able to meet with the lab boys and be instructed in the tools I'll have available to me.

GREEN

I'm sorry, Brown. Not this time.

Slowly BROWN rises from his chair. He removes a billfold from the inner pocket of his perfectly tailored suit jacket and takes out his "License to Kill." He drops it on Green's desk.

BROWN
I'm out. I have enjoyed working with you, sir.

He starts to leave.

GREEN
Come back here, Brown. Where do you think you're going?

BROWN
To Monte Carlo, for a vacation. And I think I'll take Miss Smith with me. Good day, sir.

GREEN
(blustering helplessly)
Brown! Brown!

Somehow, I don't see that scene making it onto film. So why, then, might the following scene take place in real life?

A SURGEON'S OFFICE

A SURGEON sits behind his big, comfortable desk. Important-looking medical books line the walls. YOU are seated in a chair opposite the surgeon.

YOU
Can you tell me what my surgery is going to be like?

SURGEON
We're going to put you to sleep, and when you wake up, the operation will be over.

YOU
Can't you tell me any more?

SURGEON
Just let us take care of everything.

YOU
Will I have any pain?

SURGEON

You may have some "discomfort," but there will be medication available to you afterward.

YOU

How long will it take me to recover?

SURGEON

That depends.

YOU

On what?

SURGEON

Oh, on a lot of things.

YOU

Can't you give me more specific information?

SURGEON

The nurses in the hospital will tell you everything you need to know.

YOU

But ...

SURGEON
(cheerily)

Don't worry. Everything will be fine. See you in the OR.

A bit fanciful, perhaps. But the point is valid. A secret agent would want to be as familiar as possible with every challenge facing him before taking on an important mission. Similarly, you should be aware of everything you will experience before, during, and after your surgery so that you will be that much better prepared to come through your operation with the greatest possible success and comfort.

Logical as this seems, there is also good scientific evidence to support the importance of preoperative information in assisting recovery. Dr. Erling A. Anderson and his colleagues from the University of Iowa demonstrated this in a study comparing the surgical outcomes of different groups of patients undergoing cardiac surgery.

One group of patients received full information about their upcoming operations, including detailed descriptions of what procedures they would undergo and the sensations they were likely to experience. Other patients were informed about routine hospital procedure, but were given no details on exactly what they would be experiencing.

The patients who received the detailed information had less anxiety about their surgery and a greater belief in their ability to control their recoveries. Even more important, the incidence of the postoperative complication of high blood pressure was about one-third less in the well-informed group. So having information about what you are going to experience will make you less anxious about your surgery and may even lower the risk of some postsurgery complications.

Remember what Francis Bacon said: Knowledge is power. The more you know about your surgery beforehand, the more power you will have to control certain aspects of it and contribute to a successful outcome.

I've divided the information into three parts. First, we'll discuss events that take place preoperatively, right up to the moment you enter the operating room. Then we'll examine what you will actually experience in surgery. Don't think that just because you'll be anesthetized, goings on in the OR (operating room) won't affect you. They certainly can, and I'll tell you what you can do while the surgical team is operating. (Believe me, this is not as nutty as it sounds!) Finally, we'll discuss the recovery period and what you can do to accelerate your recovery.

Preoperative

As I said at the beginning of this book, you have probably already decided to have surgery, so I'm not going to spend time advising you regarding surgical and nonsurgical options. I presume that you have already had such discussions with your personal doctor and the surgeon. If you haven't, though, or if you are still unsure about proceeding with surgery, I strongly suggest that you make an appointment with your doctor to discuss your concerns and have your questions answered. Be sure you have a good understanding of exactly what is going to be done. Ask about recovery time and potential complications. In Chapter 4 we'll discuss further how to approach these issues with your surgeon.

Notice, by the way, that I said *potential* complications. Surgery is very safe, and the chance of anything untoward happening to you is very small. It's important to remember that everything in life has potential complications. Driving to the grocery store, for instance. There are minor potential complications such as flat tires and parking tickets, but there can also be major ones such as hitting a telephone pole. However, driving is something many of us do every day, so we tend not to think about all the bad things that could happen to us behind the wheel of a car. Surgery is not something we do every day, so the potential problems loom larger in our minds.

PREOP MEDICAL EVALUATION

It is the concern of everyone involved in your surgery that you come through it safely. The more information the doctors and nurses taking care of you have about you and your health, the better the job they will be able to do. Consequently, several times before your surgery different people will ask you about your health and examine you. These include your personal physician, the surgeon, the anesthetist,* nurses, and the hospital resident physicians.

The first person who will perform a complete evaluation will be your personal physician. This examination is often referred to as a medical clearance. Its purpose is to establish the status of your health and your fitness for surgery. You may think your doctor knows this already and does not need to go through it again. She in fact may have most of the data she needs, but the information must be absolutely up-to-date before you have surgery.

If your personal doctor is not on the staff of the hospital where you are having your operation, the hospital may require that the medical clearance be performed by a physician who is on its staff. In that case, either the surgeon or your own doctor can refer you to a physician to perform the clearance.

Having to make the acquaintance of a new physician may seem like an unnecessary inconvenience and expense to you, but the hospital reasons that it is assuming responsibility for your care and it therefore needs to be able to rely on the competence of the person clearing you. This is not to say that the hospital does not regard your own physician as competent, but rather that the hospital simply doesn't know her.

The Medical History

Be ready to answer a slew of questions. Many people think that the most important part of a doctor's exam is the actual hands-on examination itself. Not so. About seventy percent of a doctor's information about you comes from *your answers* to her questions (the medical history). Twenty percent comes from the physical examination. Only ten percent of the infor-

---

*A word about terminology. By "anesthetist" I mean the person who will actually administer your anesthesia. This may be an anesthesiologist (a physician trained in the specialty of anesthesia) or a nurse-anesthetist.

mation comes from tests. So please be patient with all the questions, whether the physician asks you directly or has you fill out a questionnaire.

Your doctor or the doctor clearing you will ask you about any operations you may have had previously and any difficulties you may have encountered. She will also ask about any hospitalizations for other reasons and any major illness you have had. There are several areas of particular concern.

Your heart, lungs, and blood vessels are vitally crucial during surgery to deliver oxygen and nutrients throughout your body, so the doctor will be especially interested in any problems you may have had with these crucial organs. She will further inquire about high blood pressure and diabetes, since complications of these diseases can affect how you respond to surgery.

The doctor will want to know if you have had any problems with your thyroid gland since it plays a crucial role in your body's metabolism (the speed at which your "motor" runs, if you will). Also of great importance is whether you have ever had any problems with your blood clotting properly, for instance if you have bled excessively after dental work.

The physician will also perform what is called a "review of systems." This is a series of "Have-you-ever-had . . . ?" and "Do-you-get . . . ?" questions inquiring into many aspects of your health, including a history of headaches, your bowel and urinary habits, whether you suffer from back problems or arthritis, if you have ever had a blood clot in your legs, and seemingly countless other questions. Don't worry. Your answer to most of these inquiries will be no, you've never had any of these problems. (I have always thought that there are two ways to regard this list of questions: If you are an optimist, you say to yourself, "Hey, I guess I'm pretty healthy." If you're a pessimist, you say, "Gee, look what's waiting for me!")

Medications and your reactions to them are another important area into which the doctor will inquire. You should tell her if you have ever had a bad reaction to *any* medicines you have taken, either prescription or over-the-counter. Also, have a complete list of all medications you take regularly, including the exact doses and frequencies at which you take them. Do this even for your own personal physician. Even the best doctors' medication lists can get out-of-date for individual patients. If you are not sure of exactly what you take, bring all your prescription bottles with you.

Your lifestyle has a major effect on your health, so expect several questions on that subject. Do you smoke? If not, did you smoke in the past? When did you quit? If you do smoke, how much? For how long? Do you drink alcohol? How much? How often? Under what circumstances? How much exercise do you get? What kind? How often? For how long?

It is crucial that you answer these questions as honestly as possible. For instance, it is especially common for people to underestimate how much they drink. Understand that the doctor asking these questions is not passing judgment on you. This is simply information she needs to have to evaluate how you'll tolerate surgery.

The Physical Examination

Every doctor examines patients a little differently. They are all taught the same basic techniques, but over the years they change them a bit to suit their individual styles. It's sort of like how you learned penmanship in school. You were taught to form the letters in a standard way, but over the years your handwriting has taken on your own unique characteristics. What follows is a general description of how you will be examined, but remember that the actual exam will vary a bit from doctor to doctor.

The doctor will count your pulse either by feeling your inner wrist with her fingers or by listening to your heart with the stethoscope. She will also take your blood pressure. She will wrap an inflatable cuff around your upper arm and pump up the cuff with a rubber bulb. As the cuff tightens on your arm, the pressure may make your arm throb uncomfortably for ten to fifteen seconds. The doctor will then slowly release the pressure in the cuff as she listens with her stethoscope to your pulse at the crook of your elbow. She is listening for when she first hears your pulse (the upper, or systolic, number) and then when she can no longer hear the pulse (the lower, or diastolic number).

The upper number represents the amount of pressure your heart produces when it squeezes to pump your blood. The lower number is the amount of pressure left over in your blood vessels when the heart is relaxing between pumps. We like the numbers to be less than 140/90. It is perfectly acceptable to ask the examining physician what your blood pressure is.

The doctor will also examine your head, eyes, ears, mouth, and throat. The eye exam is especially important. The doctor is looking at the tiny blood arteries and veins in the back of the eyes; and these give a pretty good clue as to the status of tiny blood vessels elsewhere in the body. The effects of high blood pressure, diabetes, and hardening of the arteries, all of which can damage blood vessels in your vital organs, can be detected in the eyes.

Working down through your body, the doctor will check your neck and might examine your thyroid gland, in the front of your neck. This sometimes involves a little digging around with the fingers and can cause minor discomfort. The examiner may also listen with her stethoscope to the large blood vessels in the neck that carry blood up to your brain.

Next come the lung and heart exams. The doctor will probably thump lightly around on your back by resting one or two fingers on your back and tapping them with the other hand. This procedure, called percussion, tells the doctor the size of your lungs and if there is fluid around the lungs that doesn't belong there. Quite frankly, this information is better revealed by a chest X-ray, but percussion is a time-honored technique, and everyone still does it.

Then you will be asked to take some deep breaths in and out slowly through your mouth. As you do this, the physician will be listening with her stethoscope to how air is flowing in and out of your lungs and checking for any abnormal sounds that could indicate a problem. If the lung exam goes on long enough, or if you breathe too rapidly, you may start to feel light-headed. If this happens, inform the doctor and return to normal breathing for a minute or two.

During the heart exam, which comes next, you should simply resume normal breathing. As the doctor moves the stethoscope around your chest, she is listening to different structures in your heart and how the blood flows through them. In many cases, she will ask you to change your position as she listens.

The examination of your belly ("abdomen," if you want to sound official) has several different parts. After studying your abdomen's contour, the doctor will listen to it with her stethoscope. She is listening for the normal passage of food and gas through the intestines. Then she will percuss your abdomen, and by the sound her tapping makes be able to estimate the size of your liver and check for the presence of abnormal amounts of gas. Finally, she will press around your abdomen with her hands, gently at first and then more deeply, feeling for abnormalities of the organs and checking for tenderness in any area. She will also probably press up under your rib cage on the right side to feel the liver. This can cause some mild discomfort.

The physician will also check your arms and legs, perhaps feeling for pulses in different areas and pressing hard with her fingers on your lower legs to check for the presence of swelling there.

She may also perform a detailed examination of your neurologic (brain and nervous system) functions. This might entail watching you walk, testing your coordination and muscle strength, and touching you with a pin, tissue, or vibrating tuning fork to check your ability to feel different types of sensation.

Many hospitals require a genital and rectal examination for patients undergoing surgery. Not only is the doctor checking for internal abnormalities, but also for the presence of hidden blood in the stool.

Patients, understandably, find the genital and rectal exams embarrassing. At the risk of being crude, let me just say that, from the doctor's point of view, this is a classic case of "if you've seen one . . ." To the doctor who has examined hundreds or thousands of people, no part of your body is different from another. However, a sensitive physician will take care to respect your modesty during these exams.

Some people are concerned that a rectal examination will be painful. This is by no means necessarily the case, particularly if the physician proceeds slowly. You will find it helpful to take slow, deep breaths in and out during a rectal exam. This helps to relax the sphincter muscle at the entrance to the anus and lessens discomfort.

Finally, the physician may pay particularly close attention to the part of the body that is to be operated on. Be sure to inform her if this area is especially sensitive to being touched or moved so that she can take extra care to minimize any discomfort to you from the exam.

Laboratory Tests

Every hospital requires certain blood tests, and most require a chest X-ray and an electrocardiogram (ECG) prior to surgery. In some cases these will be performed in the office of the physician performing the medical clearance. Often, particularly if surgery is not being performed as an emergency, the hospital will ask you to come there several days before your scheduled operation to have the tests taken.

Having blood drawn is a mildly uncomfortable procedure. The doctor, nurse, or technician who does it will first place a rubber tourniquet around your upper arm. The tourniquet is placed tightly enough that blood can continue to be pumped into your arm through your *arteries* but can not run out of your arm through your *veins*. The effect of this is to cause your veins to become engorged with blood, so that they are easy to see and to pierce with a needle. The tourniquet will also make your arm throb and feel tense.

After the vampire—sorry, the blood drawer—places the tourniquet and finds a suitable spot to take the blood (usually in the crook of your elbow), he will clean off the skin with alcohol and then insert a needle under the skin and into a vein. The best way I can describe this is to say that it feels like a needle going into your arm. He will then withdraw several tubes of blood before releasing the tourniquet and withdrawing the needle. He will probably put some cotton over the puncture site and tell you either to press down on the cotton or to fold your arm in tightly. The purpose of this is to prevent blood from leaking out of the vein into the surrounding tissues. If this happens, within a short time you will have a mildly painful black-and-blue mark that lasts for a few days. To prevent this, be sure to hold the area firmly for about three minutes after the needle is withdrawn.

These days everyone who draws blood is specially trained in techniques to prevent the spread of blood-borne diseases such as hepatitis and AIDS. They wear gloves and follow carefully defined procedures. Nevertheless, if you know you have a potentially contagious blood disease, it would be a very generous courtesy for you to inform anyone who handles your blood. I know they would appreciate it greatly.

The blood tests the hospital requires will check you for a large variety of problems that could affect your surgery. These include anemia (insufficient red blood cells to carry oxygen to your body), imbalances of electrolytes (sodium, potassium, and other elements that are vital to the functioning of your nerves and organs), problems with the liver's and kidneys' abilities to cleanse your blood of waste, and failure of your blood to clot properly. These are things your surgeon needs to know about before the operation begins.

A chest X-ray also provides valuable information, particularly regarding the health of your heart and lungs. The hospital will almost certainly require one if you are to undergo anesthesia. Many times, if you have had a chest X-ray somewhere else within the last several months, the hospital will accept a copy of those films in lieu of a new X-ray. However, even if you should have to take a new one, do not be concerned with the potential harm of added X-ray exposure. The amount of radiation in a single chest X-ray is only one-hundredth of what you should be exposed to over the course of a year. Furthermore, the information gained by studying your chest film far outweighs the negligible risk from having it taken.

When you have your chest X-ray taken, you will have to remove any clothing and jewelry from your waist up to your neck. You will receive a cloth or paper gown to wear. The technician will also place a lead apron on you to protect your genitals. *If you are a woman, be sure to tell the technician if there is any chance of your being pregnant.*

The technician may first measure the width of your chest to determine the proper setting for the X-ray camera. He will then position you facing a metal holder containing the actual X-ray film. You will be asked to place your hands on your hips and hold that position while the technician aims the camera. Next he will step behind a lead partition and instruct you to take a deep breath and hold it. You will hear a short beep, after which the technician will tell you that you may relax. Please be sure to resume breathing.

The technician will replace the film holder with a different one and then position you with your left side against it. You will be asked to reach up toward the ceiling with both arms and once again hold your breath as a picture is taken from this new angle.

I often tell my patients that these two views make the chest X-ray sort of a medical mug shot. One day, though, a patient came into my office who was reputed to be involved in organized crime. I decided that this small joke would probably not amuse him.

The final test that is performed as part of the medical clearance is the electrocardiogram, or ECG. This gives important information about the electrical activity of your heart as well as the heart muscle itself. Your heart beats by generating its own tiny electrical impulses that travel through the heart, causing the heart muscle to contract and pump out blood. You will lie comfortably on a table as the technician places four recording electrodes attached to wires on your arms and legs and another six across your chest. She may use self-adhesive electrodes or have electrodes that look like little suction cups. If she uses the suction cups, she will also put some conductive cream on your chest to help them stick better. The technician will then record your electrocardiogram on a machine that produces a paper tracing of your heart's activity.

Remember, the ECG is measuring your heart's electrical activity, not sending any electricity into you. You will feel absolutely nothing while the test is being taken.

The Results

The vast majority of the time, nothing will turn up on your preoperative clearance examination that will jeopardize your having surgery. Should the doctor find something questionable, however, it is far better that it be discovered and dealt with before your operation than during it. Consequently, before clearing you, the doctor may want you to have some additional evaluation. If this is the case, be sure you get a clear explanation of what the problem is and what the physician wants done. It may be, for instance, that your ECG shows an abnormality that concerns the doctor but that you have known about for years. A few minutes of discussion will often clear up any such minor problems. If questions still remain, the doctor performing the preoperative evaluation should discuss her findings with your personal physician, if they are not one and the same person.

The Internist's Continuing Role

The physician who performs your medical clearance should continue to see you in the hospital after your surgery to assist in your postoperative care. Most surgeons will welcome the internist's input, whereas some others may feel that they can handle any eventuality themselves. Frankly, common sense suggests that two medical heads would be better than one and that the internist can play a valuable role in postoperative management. A recent study of patients undergoing cardiothoracic (heart and/or lung) surgery confirms common sense. In cases where the internist played an active role after surgery, patients had fewer complications, fewer lab and X-ray tests, and thirty percent shorter hospital stays. So encourage your internist to see you daily after your operation; it will be worth the modest extra expense.

DONATING YOUR OWN BLOOD

Here is an excellent example of a step in the surgical process where you can have some control over your treatment. It is unavoidable that patients do lose some blood during surgery, the amount depending on the type of operation. Later, you will learn some mind-body exercises that can actually lessen the amount of blood you lose. However, you can also predonate your own blood, to be held in storage for you should you require a transfusion during or after surgery. Then your own blood will be given back to you.

You can start banking your blood as long as six weeks before the date of surgery and predonate as often as every four days right up to seventy-two hours before the operation. In most cases, you will give two to four units (pints), one unit at a time.

Donating blood is not much different from having blood drawn for blood tests, except that the needle used is larger and it stays in your arm longer. Also, the tourniquet does not stay on your arm the whole time, so your arm does not throb for the twenty or so minutes that donating takes. You will sit in a reclining chair with your arm on an armrest, and the blood-bank technician will insert the needle into your arm. The blood flows from your arm through a plastic tube to a collection bag next to you. The bag rests on a rocking device on the floor. The constant motion of the bag helps to keep the blood from clotting. New, sterile equipment is used for each donor, so there is no risk of your acquiring an infection from the blood donation process.

After you donate, you will probably be asked to remain in a reclining position for several minutes. If you get up prematurely, you may feel dizzy. To avoid this, first swing your legs over the side of the chair and let them dangle for a minute or two before you stand up. The technician may also offer you some juice. If you continue to feel dizzy, you will be welcome to remain there as long as you need to.

During the weeks that you are donating your own blood, your doctor will probably prescribe iron pills to help your body make new blood cells to replace those that are withdrawn. Alternatively, the doctor may give you injections of epoetin alpha (Epogen or Procrit) to stimulate your body to produce new red blood cells. Epoetin is a synthetically made version of a natural body hormone. It is safe to use and virtually free of side effects.

Ask your surgeon if donating your own blood ahead of time is appropriate to your situation so that you can make arrangements with the hospital.

CHECKING IN TO THE HOSPITAL

Your surgery may or may not require your being admitted to the hospital. Many operations are performed on an "ambulatory" or "outpatient" basis. You come in, have the surgery, and go home a few hours later. Hernia repairs and cataract surgery are two of the types commonly performed this way.

More complicated surgery will require admission to the hospital for a stay of one to several days. The hospital will inform you ahead of time when and where to come for admission. In the past, patients were generally admitted the day before surgery. Now, to save expenses, you may be asked to come in very early on the day of your surgery.

Making the Hospital More Hospitable

Hospitals are strange and foreign places to most of us, but you can make the hospital environment more friendly to you. Remember those Swedish commuters who were able to make their long train rides less stressful by arranging their things and getting comfortable at the beginning of the ride? You can similarly improve your hospital environment by bringing some personal things with you to make your hospital room more homey and familiar.

In addition to your personal toiletry items, bring along your own pajamas, robe, and slippers. Don't go out and buy new ones to impress hospital personnel; they won't be impressed. Bring your old, beat-up, comfortable ones. Be sure to have some family pictures in small frames to put on your bedside table; it's comforting to have them always around.

Bring a teddy bear. You'll find out why later.

You probably will not have much choice as to the room you

will be staying in. Hospitals assign rooms as they become available. If you should have a choice, though, try to get a room with a window that looks out on an open area. A famous study some years ago showed that surgical patients whose hospital room window faced an open area recovered more quickly than those whose window looked out on a brick wall. In any case, you may want to bring a poster of a beautiful nature scene to hang on your wall to bring nature indoors. Some people also like posters with inspirational sayings on them.

The goal is to create a mini-environment within the hospital where you will feel comfortable and secure. (But try not to clutter up the place too much!)

As we'll discuss shortly, I highly recommend that you bring with you a portable Walkman–type personal tape player with headphones and fresh alkaline batteries. You are going to be listening to music during your operation.

One more thing. We'll discuss this further in the next chapter, but I also suggest you bring with you a small gift for the hospital staff when you enter the hospital. Patients sometimes leave a thank-you gift when they are discharged. It's always struck me that by then it's a little too late.

Incidentally, don't bring any valuables with you. Leave your jewelry at home and bring only enough money for incidental expenses such as newspapers. Unfortunately, personal items can occasionally grow legs of their own and walk out on you.

Admission Procedures

At the admitting office, a member of the staff will register you and take information about your insurance and place of employment. Bring your social security number and insurance cards with you. You will also sign a few consent forms giving the hospital and doctors permission to treat you. Don't be concerned if you are asked if you have a living will or if you have selected a health-care proxy (a person to make medical decisions for you if you are unable to make them for yourself). These questions have become routine hospital procedure in many places.

If you are lucky, you will not have to wait too long for your assigned bed to be ready for you, and a member of the hospital staff will escort you to your room. Once you are there, the nursing staff will help you to settle in and then take a medical history of their own. They will ask you about any prior operations or illnesses you might have had and get a list of medications you take. They will probably also perform a brief examination. Next they will familiarize you with the routine hospital procedures such as mealtimes and visiting hours. They will also teach you certain breathing exercises that you will have to do after surgery. (More on that later.)

What? Another Exam?

Depending on your individual hospital, the next person to visit you will probably be either a physician's or surgeon's assistant or a surgical house officer (intern or resident). He will take yet another complete medical history and perform a thorough examination.

At this juncture a few questions might come to your mind: "Can't they just ask my doctor or get all this information from my chart?" Or, worse: "Is this hospital using me as a guinea pig for their young doctors to learn on?" The answers to both these questions is an emphatic "No!"

Medical care in a hospital, as opposed to your doctor's office, entails a team approach. Many people have different tasks, all of which contribute to your final outcome. What you want is for them to be thinking about you *independently*, not relying on each other for information. Otherwise, errors can easily creep into the picture.

Suppose, for instance, that you forget to mention to your surgeon that you have an allergy to penicillin. If every other person who looks after you simply reads the surgeon's notes about you, none of them will be aware of your allergy. One of them could order penicillin for you with disastrous consequences. It's far better to have each person ask you your allergies independently; that way misinformation is less likely to slip through.

Regarding the interns and residents, I must confess that with each passing year they look younger and younger to me. I can easily understand your concern about having a "kid" taking care of you. Keep in mind that these "kids" are graduate physicians who are taking specialty training. They are working under the direct supervision of your surgeon, and they continually consult with him regarding any decisions that affect your care. They will be in the operating room with you and will assist your doctor with the surgery. (Despite stories you might have heard, it is your surgeon who will be doing the operation.)

You should know that you do have the right to refuse examination by a resident. I can't recommend it, though. Remember that your doctor cannot be in the hospital with you twenty-four hours a day. Should an urgent problem arise at 3 A.M., the resident will be the first physician there to help. The more he knows about you and (human nature being what it is) the more he feels involved with your care, the more help he can offer. The residents and physician's assistants will often have more time to spend with you than will your doctor. They are good people to have on your side.

The Anesthesiologist

Modern anesthesia has made great strides in even the past ten years, greatly increasing the safety and reducing the side effects of anesthesia. We will discuss this a little later when we head into the operating room.

Before your operation, the person who will be administering your anesthesia will discuss it with you. He will once again take a medical history and perform a brief examination. He will pay special attention to your mouth and neck, as these will be the particular areas he will be working with. Be sure to tell him if you have any removable dentures or crowned or loose teeth. It is also important for you to tell him if you have had any prior experience with anesthesia and if you had any difficulty with it. Any bad experiences blood relatives have had with anesthesia are also important information to give.

The anesthesiologist will make his own assessment as to whether it is safe for you to undergo surgery and anesthesia. He may discover something that the other doctors who have evaluated you have not. He has the right, if need be, to cancel your surgery even if this inconveniences you and the surgeon. This is quite unlikely, but if it should occur, try not to be angry. Your safety and comfort are the anesthesiologist's primary concerns. He will do whatever he has to to maximize them.

Presuming that all systems are "go," the anesthesiologist will explain the type of anesthesia you are having and answer any questions you might have. As will be discussed further on, you may have the opportunity to choose the type of anesthesia you want. This is a good time to mention to him that you want to listen to music during your operation and get his permission to bring your tape player into the operating room.

Finally, take this opportunity to discuss with the anesthesiologist medications for pain control after surgery. (You'll learn more about this shortly, too.)

SURGICAL PREPARATION

Your particular preparation for surgery will depend on the type of operation you are having. The nurses will probably be the ones to explain exactly what will be done. Here are some general guidelines:

- Eating and drinking. Your stomach needs to be completely empty before surgery. Otherwise, partially digested food and stomach acid can back up into your throat and go "down the wrong pipe" into your lungs. This would result in aspiration pneumonia, an extremely serious complication. The general rule of thumb is that you will be given nothing to eat or drink for several hours before surgery. If you are having your procedure as an outpatient, you should also adhere to this policy unless otherwise instructed.

• Shaving: Until recently it was standard surgical procedure to shave off any body hair at the site where the surgical incision was to be made. The rationale for this was that it made it easier to sterilize the skin before cutting into it. It turns out that shaving can actually increase the risk of a wound infection, so many surgeons will not shave your skin unless the hairs interfere with sewing you up.

• Skin marking: It is not uncommon for the surgeon or one of his assistants to mark your skin precisely where they will be doing the cutting. This may be done the night before or immediately before the operation. The ink does not wash off easily, so you may still bathe once you have been drawn upon.

• Bowel preparation: Some types of intestinal surgery require that the intestines be entirely empty of food and stool. There are two main ways to accomplish this. One is to restrict your diet and give you powerful laxatives and enemas starting two days before your surgery.

Another approach is to have you drink a cleansing solution (Colyte or Golytely) the day before. This is about a gallon of clear slightly salty or fruit-flavored solution that you drink over the course of a few hours. You have to drink an eight-ounce glass every ten minutes to get the full effect. The stuff is more palatable if you drink it through a straw.

Initially, you may get some abdominal cramping, and if the solution was refrigerated, you might feel quite cold. After an hour or so of drinking, you will start to have frequent, loose bowel movements, which will continue until only clear liquid is running out of you. As you are drinking, you may well think to yourself, "There must be a better way." Unfortunately, drinking the solution is the better way.

On the day before abdominal surgery you will also receive oral antibiotic medications to reduce the number of bacteria in your intestines. This helps to reduce the incidence of infection after surgery.

- Sleep medication: I have never been a big proponent of sleeping pills. Frankly, I hope that with the self-relaxation exercises you will have been doing, you will be nice and calm the night before your surgery and not need anything to help you get to sleep. However, even with the best preparation you might have difficulty falling asleep. It is not a failure on your part to ask for a sleeping pill. In fact, it is so common for people to need one that sleep medication orders are generally included in standard admitting orders.

THE DAY OF SURGERY

You will be awakened early and be given the opportunity to go to the bathroom and get washed up. In some cases you will be asked to shower with a special cleansing soap. You may brush your teeth, but don't drink any water. You will receive a fresh hospital gown to wear instead of your own pajamas.

It is generally acceptable to hospitals and nursing staffs for one or two members of your family to be with you now, even if you are going to the operating room before regular visiting hours begin.

Even in the best hospitals a tray of food may arrive from the kitchen for you. DON'T EAT IT! As noted above, your stomach must be empty for you to have surgery. If someone brings you food, it means either that a mistake has been made or that your surgery has been canceled for that day. If you do eat, you can be very sure that your surgery will be canceled! You may, however, take oral medications with a sip of water before surgery.

Premedications

You may receive two types of medications immediately prior to surgery, antibiotics and sedatives. Not every operation requires antibiotics beforehand. If you need them, you will generally receive them intravenously about an hour before you are called to the operating room or, in many cases, right in the OR. Their purpose is preventative, to lower the risk of acquiring an infection during surgery.

A nurse, physician, or IV specialist will start your intravenous line, most likely in a vein in the back of your hand. He will clean your skin with alcohol or an iodine solution and place a tourniquet on your arm to allow the veins to become engorged with blood. The IV catheter itself is a hollow plastic tube with a metal needle going up the middle. It does hurt some when it is inserted. (The person starting your IV will probably mumble something like "a little pinch now" when he strikes. Frankly, it's not little and it's not a pinch, but it is tolerable.)

The technician will tape the IV catheter in place and connect it to a bag containing a salt/sugar/water solution. This serves to keep your vein open. The nice thing is that once the IV line is in you, you can receive intravenous medications repeatedly without having to undergo further sticks.

If you do not require antibiotics in advance, your IV will be started in a holding area where you will wait to go into the operating room. There the anesthetist who starts the IV will often give you a local anesthetic to numb your skin before inserting the needle.

The anesthesiologist who is handling your surgery may have ordered sedatives to be given to you prior to coming to the operating room. These induce a pleasant state of calm before surgery, and I recommend you take these medications even if you have done all the mental preparation exercises I suggest. The more you have going for you, the better.

You will receive these premedications through an injection. They will make you feel drowsy and relaxed and may even cause you to forget much of what happens. That's fine. You may also receive a medication (Robinul) that causes body secretions to dry up. If so, you will experience a dry mouth and perhaps blurry vision.

Finally, many anesthesiologists administer medications to

reduce the amount of acid in your stomach and/or help your stomach to empty faster. You should not notice any significant side effects from these drugs.

To the OR

A hospital attendant will help you to lie down on a gurney (stretcher on wheels) and will take you to the operating room (OR). You will most likely go first to a holding area right outside the operating room itself. You will be aware of a bustle of activity as the nurses and OR technicians prepare the OR for your operation. You will also see your anesthesiologist, though it may be hard to recognize him behind his surgical mask.

ANESTHESIA

The Risk of Anesthesia

One of the things that people fear most about surgery, and one area where they feel they have the least control, is anesthesia. Let me tell you why these fears are unfounded.

The general approach to anesthesia has changed drastically over the past several years. The goals of anesthesia are to make you unconscious and insensitive to pain, to cause your muscles to relax completely, to suppress your reflexes, and to cause you to forget everything that has happened.

In the past, all these goals were achieved with large doses of a single, potentially dangerous drug. Now, however, anesthesiologists use combinations of several medications in small doses to get the same effects. The use of small doses makes it safer to use each drug. Furthermore, the technology available to administer anesthesia, as well as to monitor your vital functions during anesthesia, is more sophisticated than ever before. Consequently, the risk from anesthesia is negligible.

You might be thinking, "That's what you say, but I read in

the paper where some guy had anesthesia and . . ." To which I reply that the reason such a story even makes the newspaper is that serious anesthetic mishaps are rare enough to be newsworthy. By way of comparison, you will notice that newspapers seldom report how many airline passengers arrive safely at their destinations every day.

Types of Anesthesia

Several different types of anesthesia are available, depending on the particular operation to be performed. Your anesthesiologist will discuss with you what type she recommends for your surgery. Here is a brief summary of the different types of anesthesia, including what you actually feel, starting with the least invasive.

Local: Anesthesiologists refer to this as MAC (monitored anesthesia care). It entails injection of a numbing drug right into the site of operation, blocking the nerves from sending pain messages to the brain. If you've gotten a "shot" in your mouth before having dental work done, you've had local anesthesia. In the surgical setting, local anesthesia is commonly combined with the intravenous administration of sedative drugs to relieve anxiety, reduce discomfort, and induce amnesia for the procedure.

If you have local anesthesia, you will first receive a sedative medication that will make you feel calm and drowsy. You probably won't care very much about what is going on. When the actual local is administered, you will first feel "a little pinch" when the needle is introduced, followed by a few seconds of stinging at the point of injection. Then you will feel nothing.

The great advantage of local anesthesia is that while the area operated on is completely numb, the rest of your body is unaffected. Local anesthetic drugs have minimal, if any, effect on your heart, breathing, blood pressure, and other vital body functions. After the operation, the anesthesiologist will keep a careful eye on you while the sedative drug wears off. Once you are fully awake, can take fluids by mouth, and have urinated, you will be able to go home.

Local anesthesia is commonly used where only a very discrete area of the body needs to be numbed, such as removal of growths from the skin, cataract surgery, vasectomy, and some hernia repairs.

Regional: With this technique, a large area of the body, say from the waist down, is numbed by injecting a medication around the spinal cord, which carries sensation from the body up to the brain. Different regional anesthesia techniques can also be used to numb a smaller area, say an arm or a foot. Patients undergoing regional anesthesia receive sedative medications to decrease their anxiety and awareness of the surgical procedure. There are two major types of regional block:

Epidural anesthesia involves sliding a very thin plastic tube through a hollow needle into your back until it is just next to your spinal cord. Then local anesthetic medication is gradually injected through the tube and bathes the tissues around your spinal cord. This induces numbness in your body from the point of injection downward.

Epidural anesthesia can cause your blood pressure to drop, so the anesthesiologist will often accompany an epidural with intravenous fluids to help maintain your blood pressure. The other problem with an epidural is that it sometimes induces incomplete anesthesia. This sometimes means that a different type of anesthesia must be used, although such circumstances are very rare.

A major advantage of epidural anesthesia is that the plastic tube can be left in your back after the surgery. That way, more anesthetic can be injected around the spinal cord to prevent and relieve any pain you might have after surgery.

If you choose epidural anesthesia, you will again first receive a sedative drug. Then, either you will lie on your side with your knees pulled in toward your chest or you will sit with your back arched (*Figure 3*). The anesthesiologist will first numb your skin and the underlying tissues with a local anesthetic. Again, you will feel a "pinch" and then a few moments of stinging. From that moment on, you should feel nothing but a sensation of pressure as the needle passes into your back.

Spinal anesthesia is the other method of achieving regional anesthesia. In this technique, a local anesthetic is injected right into the fluid-filled sac that surrounds your spinal cord, rather than simply around the sac, as with epidural anesthesia. Although this technique gives greater assurance of satisfactory pain relief than an epidural block, spinal anesthesia

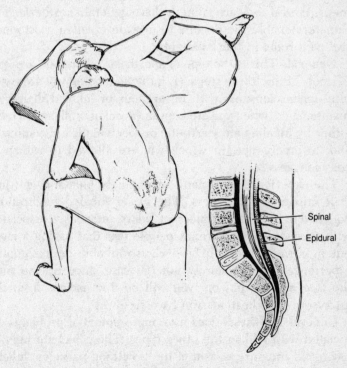

FIGURE 3

does have a higher risk of problems associated with it. These include low blood pressure, excessively rapid heartbeat, and nausea and vomiting. Some patients experience a fairly severe headache within forty-eight to seventy-two hours after spinal anesthesia. Further, a catheter is not left in to give you more medication after the surgery.

The experience of receiving spinal anesthesia is similar to that for epidural anesthesia described above.

Regional anesthesias (epidural and spinal) may be used, for instance, in patients undergoing prostate surgery, cesarean section for childbirth, and orthopedic surgery of the hips and legs. In addition, anesthesiologists will often place epidural catheters in patients having surgery on their chests or abdomens, even if they are going to have general anesthesia. The catheters enable the doctors to provide excellent postoperative pain relief in these patients.

General: This is the type of anesthesia where you are "put to sleep." It has three steps: (1) induction, when you are eased into unconsciousness with intravenous or inhaled drugs; (2) maintenance, when you are kept unconscious and comfortable either by inhaling an anesthetic or receiving it intravenously; and (3) emergence, in which you are allowed to return to consciousness.

The experience is actually surprisingly pleasant. You just drift into unconsciousness. The newer inhaled medications don't even have the unpleasant odors previously associated with such drugs. Sometimes people fear that having a mask put over their face will be a claustrophobic or frightening experience. This is simply not the case since by the time the face mask is put on, you will be unconscious from the intravenous medications you have received.

General anesthesia does have more potential problems associated with it than the other types. These include high or low blood pressure, spasm of the breathing passages, inhalation of regurgitated stomach contents (that's why you're not allowed to eat for several hours before surgery), abnormal heart rhythms, and low body temperature. However, in a recent study of seventeen thousand patients undergoing general anesthesia, the complication rate was only 0.17 percent. That means that the chance of even minor anesthesia-related problems was less than two per thousand operations.

Anesthesiologists use general anesthesia in any operation where a body cavity (chest or abdomen) is entered, when the operation is likely to take a long time, or when the use of local or regional anesthetics is not possible.

In your presurgical discussion, your anesthesiologist will discuss with you the different types of anesthesia available to you for your particular operation. He will probably recommend a specific type of anesthesia. Go with the recommendation. If you have a choice, select the less invasive form: regional rather than general, local over regional. Even with anesthesia's excellent safety record, the less you need, the better off you are.

In Surgery

Most people feel that once they are brought into the operating room, there is little for them to do. This is hardly the case. Contrary to what you might think, your brain will still be working, and your *unconscious* mind will know what is going on around you. *Even under general anesthesia you will continue to hear and your brain will continue to process information it receives.* You will not be *consciously* aware of what you are hearing, and you will remember none of it, but your brain will nevertheless be working, and things you hear can affect the outcome of your surgery!

Good proof of this has come only fairly recently, though surgeons have suspected for years that at least some of their patients could hear what was going on in the operating room even under general anesthesia. There were scattered reports in medical journals of patients making a remark after surgery about something that was said or had happened during the operation. These left the unsettling feeling that the patients had in fact registered what was going on in the OR despite being "asleep."

Thirty years ago Dr. B. W. Levinson was able to demonstrate brain wave (EEG) changes indicative of arousal in some anesthetized patients when the operating room staff staged a simulated crisis in the operating room.

More recently, Dr. Henry L. Bennett and his colleagues at the University of California have studied patients' responses to specific suggestions given to them during anesthesia. While undergoing surgery the patients heard a tape played through headphones. It had music interspersed with occasional statements that the patient was doing well and would recover rapidly. Before the end of the operation, but while still fully anesthetized, half the patients heard an additional tape during which they were given the suggestion that it would be important for them to touch their ears during an interview that would take place after surgery. The other half of the patients continued to listen to the music tape only.

The postoperative interviews took place at least two days after surgery. The patients who heard only the music tape happened to touch their ears an average of one time per interview. The patients who were told under anesthesia that it would be important to touch their ears during the interview did so an average of six times. None of the patients who were told in the OR to touch their ears had any recollection of being given that suggestion.

In summary, the patients responded to what they heard while under anesthesia even though they had no recollection of hearing it. This and similar studies indicate to me that what is said and what goes on in the operating room may affect you, even though you are completely anesthetized.

Imagine that you were having surgery under only local or

regional anesthesia, so that you were awake, and you heard your surgeon say, "Oh, my goodness. Look at this. This is terrible." You would be extremely concerned and might even panic. Your heart would probably start to race and your blood pressure would shoot up. These responses could have an adverse effect on your surgery, especially if their cause was misinterpreted by the person monitoring you.

Of course, no surgeon would make any such comment knowing that his patient was awake and listening. But suppose the operating room staff believed that the patient, being under anesthesia, was completely "out of it" and was totally unaware of OR discussions. Conversation might be a bit looser. Even an offhand remark about an unrelated subject could be harmful, say if you heard the surgeon remark, "It's the worst I've ever seen." Your brain might think he was referring to you, not the lousy movie he saw last night.

Furthermore, just the ambient sounds of the OR can be very disturbing. This is particularly the case with orthopedic surgery, where the sounds of drills, saws, and hammers make the operating room sound more like a carpentry shop.

CREATE YOUR OWN SONIC ENVIRONMENT

You cannot control what is said or the noise that equipment makes in the operating room, but you can control what you hear. This is why I recommend that you bring a portable Walkman–type tape player to the hospital with you and listen to music through headphones *during your surgery*.

The tape player you use should have an "auto-reverse" feature so that when it reaches the end of the tape it starts playing the other side. Be sure that you have fresh alkaline batteries that will not run out in the middle of your operation.

I suggest you use a tape of soothing, pleasant music, either prerecorded or assembled yourself from music you like. Many "New Age" and health food stores have a wide selection of such tapes, and oftentimes you can sample a few before purchasing one. Otherwise, check the "New Age" section in your local record store.

To enhance the effectiveness of the tape, you may add spoken suggestions to the music every five minutes or so. I'll give you the actual words to read onto your tape in a later chapter. All you have to do is record right over the music. You will erase the music for those few moments of speech, but that will not decrease the effectiveness of the tape.

If doing this seems like a lot of work to you, I have prepared a tape of soothing music and positive suggestions. (See the page at the back of the book for ordering information.)

USING THE TAPE

As a courtesy to your doctors, discuss with your surgeon and the anesthesiologist ahead of time your desire to listen to your tape in the OR. It is unlikely that either of them will object, but if they have any questions, you can refer them to medical journal articles in Part V, "Resources." Also, ask your surgeon to inform the OR nurses that he has given you permission to listen to your tape during your operation.

Use the tape regardless of the type of anesthesia you have. Before you are sedated preoperatively, set the volume control on your tape player to a level that is comfortably loud enough to block out sounds from the room. Be sure the auto-reverse feature is on. When the nurse comes to sedate you, turn on the player and ask the nurse for surgical tape that you can use to tape down the "Play" button and cover all the other controls, including the volume. You don't want any inadvertent jostling of your recorder to turn it off or switch it over to the radio, blasting static into your ears! Put on your headphones, settle back, and enjoy the music.*

---

*Incidentally, your surgeon might listen to music in the OR, too. Many surgeons find it relaxing, and a fascinating recent study showed that surgeons are less stressed and perform better when they undertake a stressful task while listening to music of their own choosing.

The next thing you know, you'll be waking up in the recovery room.

Recovery

I can no more tell you how you will feel immediately after surgery than I can predict whether you will like a particular movie you go to see. Everyone responds differently, and consequently it's hard to tell you exactly how *you* will feel. However, I can give you some generalizations that will at least give you an idea of what you are going to experience.

THE RECOVERY ROOM

You will most likely awaken in a recovery room with other patients who have just had surgery. Probably the first thing you will be aware of is one of the recovery room nurses calling your name and asking you to open your eyes or squeeze her hand. After a short while you will realize where you are.

As you return to normal consciousness, you will notice several things:

- You'll be surprised that your operation is all over and will recall nothing of what happened since you were brought into the surgical holding area.

- You will also be surprised at how good you feel. You will probably experience no pain whatsoever at the site of your surgery.

- There will be a lot more things attached to you than when you went into surgery. You may have a tube going from your nose or mouth into your windpipe. This was placed during surgery to assist your breathing. It is generally removed fairly soon after surgery.
  You may have a thin plastic tube coming out of your nose that is sucking out stomach contents. You may also have another tube coming out of your bladder to drain your urine. You will have more intravenous lines, possibly including one in your neck. In addition, there may be a thin plastic catheter in one of your arteries (probably at your wrist) to monitor your blood

pressure and take blood samples painlessly when needed. All of these tubes and lines were placed under anesthesia to spare you the discomfort associated with placement.

There may be one or more plastic or rubber tubes emerging from the gauze and tape that cover your surgical site. These are drains that allow body fluids to escape from your healing incision.

- In some hospitals your family may be allowed to visit you at this point. Give them the thumbs up.

Once the doctors and nurses in the recovery room are satisfied that your vital signs and heart and lung functions are stable after surgery, you will return to a regular hospital bed.

In some cases, for instance after particularly major surgery or if you have other medical problems, your next stop might be a surgical intensive care unit (ICU) for twenty-four hours or even a few days. Do not interpret going to an ICU as indicating that something has gone wrong. All it means is that your surgeon wants more intensive observation of you than can be provided on a regular hospital floor. For instance, some types of heart monitoring simply are not possible outside the ICU.

HOW YOU'LL FEEL

Even though I said earlier that it is impossible to tell you exactly how you'll feel after surgery, I can give you a general picture of what recovery from surgery is like.

I often tell my patients that everyone on the hospital staff is going to be very cruel to them:

- They will make you get out of bed into a chair, often as early as the day after surgery, when that's about the last thing you want to do. However, studies show that the quicker patients get out of bed and start moving about, the fewer the complications that set in.

- They will make you take deep breaths, cough deeply, and do other things to clear your lungs. For instance, they will have a device called an incentive spirometer. This is a hospital version of that carnival game where you pound a wood block with a big hammer to ring a bell.

There is a hollow, clear plastic upright stand with a plastic ball inside. Attached is a short hose with a mouthpiece. Depending on the type of incentive spirometer your hospital uses, you either blow into or inhale through the mouthpiece, trying to raise the ball as high in the plastic stand as you can. You can bet that the nursing staff will harp on you constantly to use that thing.

When you have to cough, hug a pillow or a folded up sheet against your belly. This will make it a lot easier to cough deeply. At my hospital, they give patients a cute teddy bear to hold while coughing. Now you understand why I recommended bringing a teddy bear along with your bathrobe and slippers. He's much more cuddly than a pillow or a folded-up sheet.

You might find all this coughing and inhaling and blowing to be very annoying and even uncomfortable. However, they beat the heck out of getting postsurgical pneumonia, which all these breathing exercises are designed to prevent.

- If you have had abdominal surgery, they will not let you eat or drink for a few days until your intestines start to function again.

During the few days after surgery you may experience a number of different sensations and emotions. You may very well feel *exhausted*. There are many reasons for this, including the stress of surgery itself, disrupted sleep after surgery, blood loss, and pain medication you may receive. Your energy will certainly return, but it could take several days.

Some people feel absolutely euphoric after surgery, but others experience *depression*, particularly folks who have had an open heart operation. You may even alternate between euphoria and depression. This, too, passes with time, but here is where your mental preparation will also be helpful. Later in the book you will find a script for a postsurgery tape to make for yourself. It is specifically designed to buoy your spirits and speed your recovery.

Another sensation after surgery can be *nausea*, though with the use of modern anesthetic agents this is much less common than in the past. Still, nausea is possible in people who have had operations on their abdomens. After being handled during surgery, the stomach and intestines generally shut down for a few days and do not perform their normal functions of pushing gas and digestive juices out the other end. Consequently, the stomach can expand like a balloon, causing discomfort and nausea.

Surgeons often prevent this by passing a thin plastic tube through your nose into your stomach in the operating room if you have abdominal surgery. The tube will be there when you awaken and shouldn't bother you very much. If nausea persists, there are medications to help relieve it.

If such a tube was not placed in the OR and you develop significant nausea after surgery, your doctor will place one for you. The tube is passed gently through your nose into your stomach. As awful as this sounds, the sensation is no worse than what you feel if you get water up your nose while swimming. Once the tube is in place, you will very quickly cease to notice it.

The temporary loss of intestinal function is the reason that you will be allowed nothing to eat or drink for a few days after abdominal surgery. If your mouth is dry, you will be given ice chips to suck on. When the intestines do first start to work again, you may have intermittent cramps in your abdomen. Then you will start to pass gas from the rectum. This is an important sign, which is why the hospital staff will ask you every day if you have passed gas yet. They are not being perverse.

Once you do pass gas, any tube you have draining your stomach will be removed, and you will be given clear liquids to drink. If you tolerate those, your diet will progress to soft foods and eventually back to normal. When you start to have bowel movements again, they will be loose at first and firm up in a few days.

Recent research has demonstrated that it is possible to accelerate the return of intestinal function with just the sort of mind exercises you have started learning. These are covered in detail in Part II.

If your surgery has not disrupted intestinal function, you will probably be able to eat the same or next day.

Your surgeon or his associate will visit you every day after your operation. He will examine your heart and lungs and check your surgical wound. People often fear that when he removes the bandages to look at the incision the experience will be painful. Don't worry. Surgeons recognize this and take great care in removing dressings.

There is more to the surgeon's visit than the time he actually spends with you. He will review your progress with the nursing staff, check the results of any tests you have had done, and write orders for your continuing care.

PAIN CONTROL

One of the biggest worries people express about surgery is whether they will have pain afterward. Let me tell you that *there is no reason for you to have significant pain after surgery!*

A bold statement, but true. This is not to say that people do not have pain postoperatively, but rather that *you* should not have any such pain. This is for two reasons. First, the mental-preparation exercises you have started already, plus new ones you are going to learn, will lower your discomfort level greatly. And second, you are about to learn enough about the nature of postsurgical pain that you will be able to contribute to the management of it in your case. In other words, through knowledge, you are going to control your pain. Once again, Francis Bacon was right.

Why You Hurt

What hurts one person may not hurt another. This is because pain has two components: the messages your body sends up to your brain about what's going on in your arm or abdomen or chest *and* how your brain interprets those messages. It is this individual interpretation that makes pain perception so subjective. Therefore, to learn how to control pain, we must first understand both the physical and mental components of pain.

Imagine this experiment. You take a pencil eraser and press it into your finger. You feel pressure, but certainly no pain. Now you do the same thing with the sharpened point of the pencil. You jerk your finger away and feel pain.

How do you distinguish between the dull feeling of the eraser and the sharpness of the point? In your skin are collections of nerve endings called receptors. There are different receptors for different types of sensation: pain, light touch, pressure, and temperature. Other, less well understood receptors are in the tissues underlying your skin, in your muscles, and in some organs.

When that pencil point pushes into your skin, the pain receptors send an electrical impulse along the nerves of your arm into your spinal cord, the information superhighway of nerves that runs through the middle of your spinal column. As soon as the pain message reaches your spinal cord, it sends the message on its way up to your brain and simultaneously sends another signal down the nerves to the muscles of your arm to get that finger away from there. Your body is extremely clever this way. You automatically start to withdraw your finger from the source of pain even before your brain figures out what's going on.

When the nerve impulse from the pain receptor eventually reaches your brain, it says to itself, "Hmmm. A message from one of the pain receptors. That must mean something is causing a problem down there. *Ouch!*" And you hurt.

You can now see that there are several places in this process where we can intervene to prevent pain:

1. Block the pain receptors and/or their nerves so that they don't send messages to the brain. This is how a local anesthetic works.
2. Block the spinal cord so that it does not pass pain signals along to the brain. This is what regional (spinal or epidural) anesthesia does.
3. Modify how the brain perceives the messages coming in. Generally, this is how pain medications make you more comfortable.
4. Teach the brain to ignore incoming pain signals. You have already done this in the past, for instance, if you have ever been concentrating on something so intently that you did not notice until later that you had hurt yourself. What you are going to learn later is how to do this consciously.

Several physical factors contribute to the perception of pain after surgery. First of all, you have been cut. The surgeon's scalpel has cut through and damaged nerves in your skin and muscles that send messages of sensation to your brain. Those damaged nerves send alarm signals to your brain, which it interprets as pain. Oftentimes foreign objects remain in your body—catheters, tubes, drains, IV lines, sutures, skin staples—that irritate the nerves around them. Internal organs have been manipulated. Most notably, when the stomach and intestines are handled, even in the gentlest manner, they shut down for a few days, allowing an uncomfortable buildup of fluids and gas. Furthermore, a part of your body that has been operated on may be immobilized for the first few days. It is going to object to having to start moving again.

Mind-Body Control of Pain

So there are many reasons why pain signals are going to be coming in from your body to your brain. How much pain you actually feel will depend on how your brain handles those messages. And that depends a lot on your state of mind. Emotions such as depression and anxiety can increase your perception of pain. Similarly, positive feelings will make you physically more comfortable.

What is most important for our purposes is that you can greatly affect how your brain interprets pain signals—and consequently how much discomfort you have—through simple variations of the mental exercises you are already practicing. *(You are, aren't you?)* For instance, thirty years ago, doctors at Harvard Medical School discovered that teaching patients to relax the muscles around the site of surgery greatly reduced their requirements for pain medication. You are already learning muscle relaxation. Later we will apply it to pain control.

In another study, Dr. T. T. C. McLintock and his colleagues in Glasgow, Scotland, showed that patients who were given positive suggestions on a tape they heard while under general anesthesia required significantly less morphine to control postoperative pain than did patients who did not hear the tape.

Additionally, as I touched on earlier, Dr. Henry Bennett has recently published research in which patients were able to accelerate the return of their intestinal function by about one and a half days by giving themselves specific mental suggestions to that effect.

The pre- and postsurgical scripts in Part II will give you specific exercises to help eliminate pain and speed your recovery. They put into practice what has been learned in thirty years of research.

Pain Medication

As important as your mind-body connection is in reducing postsurgical discomfort, let's not forget that you will be receiving pain medication as well. Your understanding the proper use of these drugs will greatly enhance their effectiveness for you.

Pain medication is not always used optimally. The surgical textbook *Scientific American Surgery* cites several reasons for this:

- Surgeons' and nurses' incomplete knowledge of how the drugs actually work and how to administer them.

- The use of medications on an "as needed" basis. Oftentimes orders are written to give pain medication when the patient asks for it. What happens is that the patient develops pain, decides he wants something to relieve it, asks for medication, waits for what seems like an interminable period of time, and then finds that what he is given is insufficient to relieve his pain. A classic case of too little, too late. We now know that it is much more effective to prevent pain with small doses of medication than to be forced to use larger doses once pain sets in.

- "Lack of concern for optimal pain relief." Harshly worded, but unfortunately true.

- "Failure to give prescribed medications." Nursing staffs are often overworked, and getting around to giving pain medications sometimes takes a back seat to other, more urgent tasks.

- "Fear of side effects." Properly used, pain medications can be given in smaller doses, reducing potential side effects.

- "Fear of addiction." Many of the drugs used to control pain are powerful narcotics, and for years doctors feared that giving a patient enough drugs to relieve his pain would also lead to addiction. Now that we understand pain better, we know that people simply do not become addicted to narcotics when they are used to treat acute (short-lived) pain. Postsurgical pain is generally significant for only a few days, so you will not need to take medication long enough to become addicted.

The best way to be sure that you will receive adequate pain medication is to discuss it beforehand with both your surgeon and with the anesthesiologist in his preoperative visit. Find out what you will be getting and how it will be given.

There are two main categories of pain-controlling drugs used after surgery. One group are called *non-*steroidal *anti-inflammatory* *d*rugs, or NSAIDs. These include such familiar medications as aspirin, ibuprofen, and naproxen (Advil and Aleve). In the past these could only be given orally, but a new member of the NSAID family, ketorolac (Toradol), is administered as a shot. This is particularly useful for patients who cannot take anything by mouth after their surgery.

Narcotics, especially morphine, are the other mainstay of pain control. They may be given orally, as a shot, through an intravenous line, or through an epidural catheter. They are most effective when given in small doses regularly, beginning before pain becomes a significant problem.

As I mentioned above, many anesthesiologists are now placing epidural catheters in all their patients who undergo chest or abdominal surgery. This way, the doctors can administer effective pain relief after surgery.

Milder pain medications, such as acetaminophen (Tylenol) and acetaminophen with codeine are also used.

One of the great recent advances in postoperative pain control is PCA, or *p*atient-*c*ontrolled *a*nalgesia (pain relief). Here you control when and how much intravenous morphine you get. If you have discomfort, you press a hand-held button attached to a computerized delivery device. It squirts a little morphine into your IV line to provide almost instant relief. You can push the button as often as you need, but the device is preprogrammed so that you can not overdose yourself on the drug.

Many of my patients have told me that just knowing they had direct control over the administration of their pain medication made them feel better and they believed this actually lessened the amount of medication they required. This is similar to the experience of the people in the stressful noise experiment discussed in Chapter 2. Just knowing that they could press a button to eliminate the noise made the noise that much less bothersome.

Your hospital may or may not have PCA available. If so, be sure to discuss it with your surgeon and anesthesiologist. If PCA is not used there, work out with your doctors and nurses a schedule of regular doses of pain medication so you do not have to wait for pain to become intense before getting something to relieve it.

If you have received epidural anesthesia, the catheter through which the anesthetic was administered can be left in after surgery to give you medications to keep you pain-free.

Side Effects

Let's take a moment to discuss the potential side effects of pain medications. And please note once again that I said *potential* side effects. The only side effects that really matter to you are those that you actually get. Your brother-in-law may have once gotten a rash from morphine, but that doesn't indicate that you, too, will get a rash.

The most common side effects of NSAIDs when used for postoperative pain are nausea, insomnia, diarrhea, constipation, dry mouth, and dizziness. Fortunately, these side effects are rare when the drugs are used for acute postoperative pain. There can be other problems when they are used for longer periods of time, but that should not be necessary after surgery. Morphine and its cousins can produce drowsiness, constipation, nausea, vomiting, light-headedness, and sweating. When narcotics are given through an epidural catheter, though, drowsiness is not a problem. As explained above, under these circumstances addiction is not a significant risk with narcotics, regardless of the route by which they are given.

With the mental preparation you are doing and the mental exercises you will continue to perform in the hospital, you will be able to reduce your need for pain medications, thereby lessening the chances of side effects.

Thus, with a combination of mental preparation and proper

use of pain medications, you should be absolutely comfortable after surgery.

GETTING UP, GETTING HOME, GETTING BACK TO NORMAL LIFE

How quickly you recover from surgery will depend on what type of surgery was performed and how prepared you were ahead of time. With proper mind-body preparation, including the mental exercises you have started doing (right?) and the diet and exercise regimens we will discuss, you should have as rapid and successful a recovery as can be expected for your type of surgery.

My principal guideline for recovery is to push yourself *a little bit*. The absolute worst thing you can do is to lie around in bed waiting to recover your strength. Staying in bed saps strength. The muscles quickly grow flaccid, and then getting up becomes even more difficult. So listen to those cruel nurses and get up and out of bed. If you are allowed to walk, do it a few times each day and go a little farther each time.

On the other hand, do not push yourself to the point of exhaustion. Listen to your body. If you do too much one day, you'll feel less inclined to do anything the next day. Slow, steady progress is best.

It is important to remember that the recovery from surgery is never a steady course upward:

Unlikely Chart of Progress

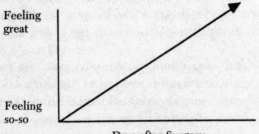

Days after Surgery

Rather, you will have good and bad days:

More Likely Chart of Progress

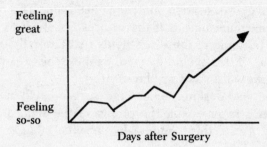

What you will notice is that improvement takes place over a several-day period. You may not feel much better on one given day than you did the day before, but you will feel better than you had a few days previously. This is comparable to watching children grow. You don't notice anything on a day-to-day basis, but if you don't see them for a while, you are surprised at how much they've grown.

You will certainly have a bad day or two along the way—a day when you feel more tired or you sleep poorly or you have less appetite. When this happens, don't panic. Just think to yourself, "Oh, that's right; Bob Baker told me this would happen," and wait till you feel better the next day.

Suture Removal

If you have sutures (stitches) or skin staples that need to be removed, your surgeon or an assistant will remove them anywhere from the fifth to tenth day after surgery. You can have the stitches removed in the surgeon's office if you go home before that. Sometimes surgeons use self-dissolving sutures that do not have to be taken out. They just disintegrate and fall out over the course of a few weeks.

Having sutures removed is not painful. The doctor will lift

the stitch up with a tweezer, slip a curved scissors under the thread, and snip it. He will then gently pull the suture material out of your skin and the underlying tissues. You will experience a tugging sensation, but no actual pain. The only time this is uncomfortable is if the sutures are stuck to the skin or hairs by some of the dried fluids that naturally ooze out of a wound. If this should happen, dabbing the area with some wet gauze will loosen up the suture.

If you have metal skin staples, the surgeon will use a plierslike device to pry open the prongs of the staples and remove them. Again, this is minimally uncomfortable.

Discharge

Your surgeon will set your date of discharge. Exactly when you go home will depend on several factors, including absence of fever or other complications of surgery, your ability to eat and move your bowels, how well you are moving about, and the healing status of your incision.

You shouldn't expect to stay in the hospital until you feel completely ready to go home. In these days of government- and insurance-company-dictated cost containment, you simply will not be allowed to convalesce in the hospital. Besides, I firmly believe that people recuperate better at home than in the hospital. You will sleep better, have better food, and have your family around.

When you are ready for discharge, have someone bring in clean clothes. This is also a good time to leave a small thank-you present for the people who helped take care of you.

If you require any medications on discharge, your surgeon or his assistant will give you prescriptions. If your hospital has an outpatient pharmacy, the person taking you home can have the prescriptions filled while you are changing into your clothes. Otherwise, go right home and have someone fill your prescriptions later for you.

The doctors and nurses will explain to you any medications you need to take as well as instruct you in any other postoperative procedures you need to do at home. Make sure you understand everything before you go. If, for instance, you need to clean your wound, make sure to do it yourself with a nurse watching to ensure that you perform the cleaning properly.

The hospital will probably require you to ride to the front door in a wheelchair. They don't want to take the risk of anything happening to you on the way out, should you not yet be strong enough to walk the whole distance out. A hospital attendant will accompany you and help you into your car.

If possible, try not to go home by yourself. The person who brings you your fresh clothes should also be prepared to drive you home or accompany you in a taxi. Don't even think about driving yourself home. You will probably be too weak to drive safely or react appropriately in the event of an emergency. Also, you will need assistance getting your things into the house. Don't be surprised if you feel completely exhausted after even a short trip home.

At Home

You may be surprised at how little energy you seem to have when you first get home. This results not only from the surgery you've had, but also from the fact that there are so many little things that you suddenly have to do for yourself. In the hospital someone brought your food right to your bedside, made your bed for you, assisted you to the bathroom, helped you to change your gown, etc. At home you'll find that doing these things for yourself will tire you out. That's fine. Keep doing them and then rest. Remember to push yourself a little bit. The last two things to return after surgery are energy and appetite. They do return, but they will take some time.

Before your discharge, your surgeon will have outlined for

you exactly what activities you may or may not engage in. Don't be embarrassed to ask specific questions about when you can walk, drive, eat, go shopping, return to work, or have sexual relations. Also be sure to arrange with the surgeon a follow-up visit at his office several days after you go home.

Finally, don't give up your mental exercises now that surgery is over. In Chapter 7 you will find a script for a postoperative tape to use after you get home from the hospital. Its goal is to speed your return to normal life. (And, you guessed it, a tape for this use is also separately available.)

By now you should have a pretty good idea of what you'll be experiencing with your surgery. You should understand the roles of the various people who will be involved in your care. And most important, you should realize that there are many places along the way where your active participation can give you some control over the surgical experience and thereby make it less stressful and more successful than you had previously thought possible.

To remind you of the things you should ask for and do, I have them in this chapter's checklist.

◆━━━━━━━━━━━━━━━━━━━━━━━━━━ ━━━━

CHAPTER CHECKLIST

Preoperative

☐ Practice self-relaxation/mental preparation; starting three to four days before surgery change to the preoperative script (Chapter 6).

THE SURGEON

☐ Discuss with your surgeon the nature of surgery, potential complications, expected recovery time.

☐ Discuss listening to a music tape during operation.

☐ Discuss postsurgical pain control, including PCA.

☐ Ask if predonating your own blood is appropriate.

PREOP MEDICAL EXAM

☐ Make a list of operations and significant medical problems you have had.

☐ Make a list of allergies to medication.

☐ Make a list of medications, including doses and frequencies, you currently take.

☐ Arrange for donation and banking of your own blood if appropriate.

THE HOSPITAL

☐ Have your social security number and insurance information handy.

☐ Remember to bring personal articles: toiletries, pajamas, robe, slippers.

☐ Bring family photos, nature poster, etc.

☐ Bring a small amount of spending money.

☐ Bring a personal tape player with headphones, fresh alkaline batteries, and a music tape.

☐ Bring a gift for hospital staff.

☐ Don't forget your teddy bear.

THE ANESTHESIOLOGIST

☐ Review prior operations and problems with anesthesia.

☐ Understand and select the type of anesthesia for your operation.

☐ Discuss listening to a music tape during surgery.

☐ Discuss postoperative pain management, including PCA.

BEFORE PREMEDICATION

☐ Set the volume on your personal tape player.

☐ Be sure the auto-reverse feature is on.

☐ Turn on the player and cover controls with surgical tape.

Recovery

☐ Use your postoperative tape (Chapter 7) to minimize pain and speed recovery.

☐ Do all the breathing and movement exercises taught by the nurses.

DISCHARGE

☐ Understand all medications and instructions.

☐ Ask questions about when you can perform specific activities.

☐ Obtain prescriptions.

☐ Have someone bring clean clothes and accompany you home.

HOME

☐ Push yourself a little bit.

☐ Make a follow-up appointment with your surgeon.

☐ Listen to home recuperation tape (Chapter 9).

☐ Congratulate yourself on having had successful surgery.

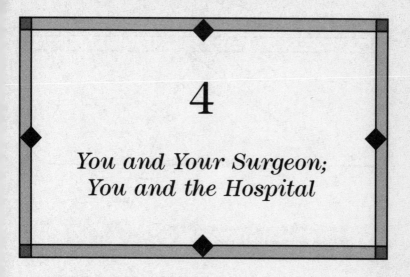

4

You and Your Surgeon; You and the Hospital

In researching this book, I came across two interesting, if opposite, views of the surgeon-patient relationship.

From poet Emily Dickinson:

> Surgeons must be very careful
> When they take the knife!
> Underneath their fine incisions
> Stirs the Culprit—*Life!*

And from Dr. George S. King, the Human Nature Chart (1934) on page 112.

It shouldn't surprise anyone that patients and surgeons have differing views of each other. After all, you want your surgeon to be the ideal surgeon:

- He is kind and gentle, with hands touched by God.

- He has only you in his appointment schedule any day you go to see him.

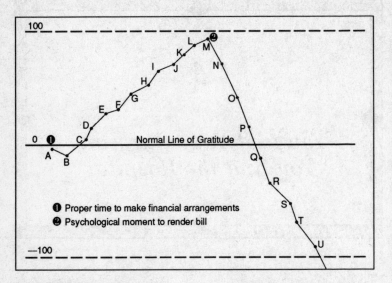

❶ Proper time to make financial arrangements
❷ Psychological moment to render bill

A	DAY OF ENTRY TO HOSPITAL	*I'm the sickest man in the world*
B	DAY OF OPERATION	*Hope I live through it!*
C	RECOVERY FROM ANESTHESIA	*So far, so good.*
D	ORANGE JUICE RETAINED	*I'm going to make the grade after all.*
E	PASSED GAS AFTER ENEMA	*Thank heaven for that!*
F	FIRST REAL MEAL	*Um-mm, that was good.*
G	FIRST SMOKE [Remember, 1934]	*What a relief!*
H	STITCHES REMOVED	*Not so bad.*
I	VISITORS	*"So I said to him...."*
J	SITTING UP	*That doctor is a wizard!*
K	BATH ROOM PRIVILEGES	*Ain't nature grand?*
L	OUT OF BED	*I'm in luck. What a doctor!*
M	ALCOHOL PERMITTED	*It certainly is great to be alive*
N	ALLOWED TO GO HOME	*I guess I wasn't as sick as I thought.*
O	WEEK AFTER	*I certainly got trimmed for that.*
P	MONTH AFTER	*Let him wait. He has plenty.*
Q	THREE MONTHS AFTER	*I don't think I needed that operation.*
R	KINDLY REMIT	*Rushing me, huh! I'll show him!*
S	PAYMENT DEMANDED	*Who the devil does he think he is?*
T	LEGAL ACTION	*Swindler! Faker!*
U	FORCED COLLECTION	*I'll tell the world what a crook he is.*
		[Nowadays: Know a good lawyer?]

- He is infinitely patient in answering your questions in language you understand.

- He welcomes any and all family members to participate in consultations.

- He is available to take your phone calls twenty-four hours a day and will drop whatever he is doing to speak with you.

- He would never dream of charging you for his services.

And he wants you to be the ideal patient:

- You are calm and accepting about the need for surgery; you don't need a second opinion.

- You are extremely concerned about his schedule and therefore try to take as little of his time as possible.

- You have no questions because you understand everything already; you are fluent in medical lingo.

- You call him only between the hours of nine and five, and it's no problem if you call him at 9 A.M. and he calls you back at 10 P.M.

- You prepay his bills.

I guess you could say these are two sets of unrealistic expectations. The purpose of this chapter is to help you forge a relationship with your surgeon based on realistic expectations and satisfaction of everyone's needs.

The Foundations of a Good Relationship

The physician-patient relationship is extraordinarily complex. It is the subject of hundreds of articles in the medical and popular literature, and it is on the mind of every physician seeing a patient. In my years of practice I have thought long and often about my relationship with my patients.

Certainly, the old doctor-as-god concept went out years

ago,* and each doctor tries to find his own way of relating to patients. Should I be formal or on a first-name basis? Do I tell them jokes, or will that seem unprofessional? Do I become emotionally involved with them or try to maintain objectivity? Do I let them control the encounter, or do I assume control? If I object to what they want, do I try to teach them or, fearing they'll go to another doctor, do I give in?

Similarly, the patient wonders how he or she should deal with the doctor. Do I ask questions, or will that seem pushy? If I think of something I forgot to ask at my appointment, can I call later, or will that make me a pest? If he keeps me waiting a long time, should I say something, or will that affect how he treats me? Will he like me better if I simply say, "Yes, Doctor," to whatever he suggests, or am I giving up too much control?

I believe that the way to resolve these dilemmas on both sides is to understand that the physician-patient relationship is dynamic and constantly evolving. It involves continual reexamination of the patient's needs and concerns and how I must respond to best meet them. Also, the patient must understand the limits of what I can accomplish, and where he must contribute.

To achieve these goals, there are two overriding principles that I think apply and that will help you with your relationship with your surgeon. First, the role of the physician is that of the hired expert adviser. Second, patient and physician will be able to make the most of that association if they share mutual respect.

THE EXPERT ADVISER

I have said to patients of mine hundreds of times: "I am your hired expert. You are paying me for my knowledge, my

---

*But if I hear that old joke that ends with the punchline, "Oh, that's God . . . He likes to play doctor" one more time, I will pull out what remaining hair I have!

experience, and my judgment. My role is to figure out your problem and then make recommendations as to how I think we can best solve it. I have to give you enough knowledge to evaluate and understand those recommendations. But it is up to you to decide how you want to proceed."

What's important is that the patient has hired me for this job. He or she is the boss; I'm the hired help. Expert help, but hired help nevertheless. An expert deserves respect, and his opinions carry the force of knowledge, but the boss must finally decide how to act.

Think of your doctor as being like an architect who is helping you design a house. You know what style you want the house to be, how many rooms it should have, and what kinds of rooms they should be. But you don't have the knowledge of structural engineering, building materials, plumbing, or electrical wiring to design the house yourself. So you hire the architect to draw up the plans. You have the right to request explanations for why things were done a certain way and then to accept or reject the plans, or request modifications of them, but at the same time, you must rely on the architect's advice.

The same is true with your surgeon. You are the master of your own health, and you must have the final say. But you simply don't have the knowledge to make a fully informed decision about what actions should be taken. You have hired the surgeon to help you understand what needs to be done and then do it.

As an expert, your surgeon deserves your respect. As his boss, you deserve his.

MUTUAL RESPECT

Ideally, mutual respect should be the basis of all human relations; unfortunately, it seldom is. It *can* be the foundation of your relationship with the people who will care for you. But you have to make it so.

It's easy to respect the surgeon. Aside from having met the rigorous standards required to gain entrance to medical school, he has continued his education for at least another five years after graduating from medical school. He has mastered the complexity of human anatomy and function and has been trained to achieve the highest degree of manual dexterity. Furthermore, he is charged with the extraordinary responsibility of repairing nature's most complex creation, the human body. You can sort of understand why some surgeons have very high opinions of themselves!

It's also easy for a lay person to feel intimidated by a surgeon. Some surgeons understand this and go out of their way to be more accessible, more human. Some others enjoy the feeling of superiority. Regardless of your surgeon's personality (and, frankly, you don't have to like him), you should have his respect in return. The best way to get it is the old-fashioned way. You earn it.

Earn respect by giving it. Remember that you and your surgeon are not adversaries. Oftentimes people come to see new doctors with a mixture of fear and suspicion. They may have heard or read somewhere that patients need to be assertive or even aggressive. They therefore go in with a chip on their shoulder and end up putting off the very person whom they are hiring to help them.

A famous story told by comedian Danny Thomas illustrates just how this happens. A traveling salesman was driving through the corn fields of Nebraska when he got a flat tire. As he went to change it, he found that the jack to raise up the car was missing. Well, he had an important customer to see, and there he was out in the country with no way to fix his flat. He looked around him and far off in the distance spotted a farm house. Hoping the farmer would have a jack he could borrow, the salesman set off across the fields for the house.

As he walked, he started to think: "I sure hope this farmer

has a jack I can use. Well, of course he will. Farmers have all sorts of equipment. He's got to have a jack.

"But if he does, will he let me use it? Country folks are friendly, so that shouldn't be a problem. Unless he doesn't like 'city slickers.' Maybe he figures I'm some rich city guy that he can take for a ride. Maybe he'll say, 'Sure, young feller, you can use my jack, but it'll cost you 50 bucks.' Or $100! Or $200!! I can't afford that!"

After another quarter mile, the salesman was getting really agitated.

"Maybe he's got this idea that I'm going to try to take advantage of his daughter. I've heard some farmers can be pretty suspicious. In fact, they're *all* suspicious. He'll probably see this as his chance to get his revenge on any salesman who ever looked twice at his fat, ugly daughter. I know he'll try to stick it to me. He'll never let me use that jack!"

Pretty soon the salesman was shouting out loud as he trudged through the corn. "I can't believe this! I'm stuck in the middle of nowhere! I'm desperate! And that rotten son-of-a-bitch is gonna make me lose this sale!"

Just then, he arrived at the front door of the farm house. He angrily pounded his fist on the door, and a few moments later a kindly looking older gentleman opened it. "Good afternoon, sir," he said. "May I help you?"

"YOU CAN TAKE YOUR GODDAM JACK AND SHOVE IT UP YOUR BUTT!!"

Like the farmer, your surgeon wants to help you. Fear and suspicion are bad emotions to bring to a new relationship. You are far better off meeting your surgeon with a positive attitude. Let him see that you want to work with him toward the mutual goal of successful surgery.

- Come to your appointment on time, but understand that he may be running late. Contrary to what people think, doctors don't keep people waiting because we have no respect for your time. It's just that things come up. Phone calls must be taken, patients require more time than planned, an operation runs longer than expected, etc. Don't get stewed while sitting in the waiting room for your appointment. If you hate waiting, you can ask the receptionist for an estimate of how long the doctor will be and take a little walk and come back. Or you could practice your self-relaxation exercises right there in the waiting room.

• Come prepared. Be knowledgeable and have a list of questions ready. More on this in a moment.

• Bring a family member or friend with you. Not only will you feel more comfortable if you are not alone, but also the other person will help you remember what the doctor says. Studies show that patients remember only about thirty percent of what doctors say to them during an office visit.

• Be patient while the surgeon does his job. He will ask you questions you may have been asked many times already. Answer fully without bringing in unnecessary details. When he examines you, show him where the problem is, so he can be gentle.

• Listen to what he says before you start asking questions. He may anticipate some of your concerns.

• Remember that he has other patients who consider their problems to be equally as important as yours. Ask how much time he has to spend with you and take only that long. If you do not feel you have been given enough time, ask when you may come back for further discussion. Since you will probably think of additional questions the moment you leave his office, ask your surgeon when might be a convenient time for you to call him back.

Coming to your appointment prepared will both show respect for the surgeon and earn his. Be ready to give him your history briefly; if he needs any details you may have left out, he'll ask. It helps to write down a few notes to remind yourself about what happened and when.

I encourage you to read as much as you can about your proposed operation *before* you see the surgeon. The more you know going in, the better you will understand what the surgeon is telling you and the better you will be prepared to ask questions. The bibliography in Part V, "Resources," lists several books written for the general public that you can purchase or take out of your local library.

Remember, though, that a little knowledge can be dangerous. Reading about your operation in a book does not equate with years of training, study, and experience. The purpose of your reading in advance is to gain understanding, not to prepare a challenge.

Finally, make a list of questions you want to ask. Most doctors welcome this. A few years ago a physician wrote a letter to the *New England Journal of Medicine* complaining about patients who came into his office with a list of problems or questions. His letter produced a deluge of responses in which doctors overwhelmingly expressed appreciation for patients who take the time to prepare for their visits by making notes. When you formulate your list of questions, do not be embarrassed that your questions may seem elementary. Remember, *the only foolish question is one that is not asked*.

WHAT YOU MAY EXPECT IN RETURN

Since you are showing respect to the surgeon, you should get it from him. As your hired expert, it is part of your surgeon's job to be sure that you understand what is going to be done and why. This will require him to spend adequate time with you and give his explanation in language you understand. If you do not feel you have been given enough time (fifteen to thirty minutes sitting with him in his consultation room should be enough), ask him to spend a little longer. If he can not, make another appointment to come back to finish your conversation. If he seems to be reluctant to give you the time you deserve, consider finding another surgeon.*

Frankly, ensuring your full comprehension of your surgery

---

*When I was in medical school, one of my instructors, Dr. Marco Zarlengo, once told me, "Remember, a doctor is like a loaf of bread. If you don't like the one you've got, take it back and get another one."

is more than just good, respectful patient care; it's the law. Your surgeon must obtain "informed consent" from you to perform the operation. When I was in my residency in the late seventies, getting consent meant shoving a piece of paper under the patient's nose and telling him to sign. Some patients would actually bother to read the paper and then ask if they were signing their lives away. We would laugh and say *no*, but the real answer was probably closer to *yes*. Fortunately, respect for patients' rights has increased since then, and the law demands that patients be given adequate information for consent to be truly "informed."

You must receive an explanation of the following:

- The nature of the procedure; that is, exactly what is going to be done.

- The expected benefits to you. How will you be better off after surgery than you were before.

- The risks of the operation. The doctor must tell you what sorts of things can go wrong with this particular type of operation. Remember, as I pointed out in Chapter 3, these are only *potential* complications. The chance of any of them happening to you is very small.

- Alternatives to the operation. I presume that you have already discussed treatments other than surgery with your personal doctor. What the surgeon needs to discuss with you is whether there are different operations available for your particular situation. For instance, there are various types of hernia repairs, each with its advantages and disadvantages.

  If alternative operations exist, the surgeon must explain to you why he is choosing a particular approach. Sometimes it will be because he has had the greatest success with a particular operation. That is a perfectly legitimate reason. As I am sure you have experienced in your own life, often what works best is what works best for you.

These four elements—nature, benefits, risks, and alternatives—comprise informed consent. One of the ways your surgeon will show respect for you is ensuring that you fully understand all of them.

Incidentally, don't be surprised if your surgeon tape records his consent discussion with you. Some malpractice insurance companies recommend this as a routine procedure to their policyholders.

Medicalese

Full understanding requires that you comprehend the language used by your surgeon. Even the most conscientious doctors will sometimes use words or abbreviations that patients are not familiar with. The reason for this is simple: we use these terms so often that they become second nature to us, and we simply forget that they are not part of every person's vocabulary.

I recently caught myself telling a patient that her chest pain was being caused by acid refluxing into her esophagus. I saw a puzzled look on her face, and in an instant realized that she had never heard the word "refluxing" before. I quickly corrected myself and said that acid was "regurgitating" into her esophagus. Still the puzzled look. So I said the acid was "backing up" into her esophagus. Still nothing. So I asked if I was making myself clear. She asked, "What's my esophagus?" It's second nature to me to use that name for the tube that carries food down to the stomach, but I was wrong to presume that a lay person would know it.

In fact, I should have remembered not to assume another person's understanding, thanks to an experience I had as a resident. A man with minimal education was admitted to the hospital with anemia (insufficient red blood cells). As part of his evaluation, I asked him if he had ever passed blood in his stool. He said, "What do you mean, my 'stool'?"

"Blood in your feces," I explained.

"What's feces?"

"Your bowel movements," I replied.

"What are bowel movements?" he asked.

Finally, I figured out how to ask the question. "Mr. L., do you ever s— blood?"

"Why didn't you say so in the first place?"

While you may not require so graphic an explanation, do not hesitate to ask your surgeon to define for you any medical terms he uses that you do not fully understand. You should not be embarrassed by asking, and your surgeon will respect you for caring enough to have complete comprehension of what he is saying.

ASKING TOUGH QUESTIONS

There are two types of tough questions: those whose answers are tough for the surgeon and those whose answers are tough for you. Be ready to ask both types.

People are reluctant to question doctors' credentials. It amazes me that in all the years I've been in practice only one person has ever called my office to ask about my credentials before becoming a patient. Not surprisingly, he was a reporter for one of the television networks. Everyone else has gotten my name from their friends, their doctor, the yellow pages, or their health plan's doctor list.

It is your right to know your surgeon's medical credentials: where he went to school and did his residency, whether he is board certified, what professional societies he belongs to. Many doctors have brochures about their practices that list their credentials. If not, you should feel free to ask him, or at least read the diplomas on his wall. If you want to know about the surgeon before walking in, you can look him up in the *Directory of Medical Specialists* in your local library. Or make it easy on yourself and call his office and ask his secretary for the information. She may react with surprise that anyone would question the "doctor's qualifications." That's okay, just be pleasantly persistent.

It is also fair for you to inquire about the surgeon's experience with your particular operation. Come right out and ask, "How many of these have you done?" Or, "How often do you perform this operation?" If the total number is less than several dozen, you should ask if yours is a particularly unusual type of procedure. If this is the case, you might want to consider having it performed at a major medical center where they have more experience with the operation.

I admit it would probably be extremely uncomfortable for you to ask a surgeon to refer you to a more experienced colleague. Your relationship with him could be tainted if you decide to stay with him. Therefore, if you are dissatisfied with his level of experience, simply tell the surgeon that you want to consider your options before making a decision. Then ask your internist for another referral.

The other type of tough questions are those whose answers might be difficult for you:

"What do you think the chance of success is?"

"Will I have much pain?"

"What will I be able to do after the surgery?"

"Can I resume my normal life?"

"When will I be able to go back to work?"

"Will I be able to have normal sexual relations?"

"What if it's cancer?"

Sometimes the honest answers to these questions will be frustratingly vague or may not be even available until the operation is over. Even then, the future is difficult to predict. Nevertheless, you are better off asking such questions and getting the issues they raise out in the open. Your fears may turn out to be worse than the reality.

Anticipation is often worse than the event itself. I find this so often in my patients undergoing surgery. They seem to presume that the worst is going to happen to them, and then their fears build up in their mind. Pretty soon, they are facing their surgery with a sense of dread. Seeing this happen again and again, and knowing it could easily be prevented, was one of the main reasons I decided to write this book. The self-relaxation exercises you are already doing *(you are, aren't you?)* will greatly reduce your anxiety.

Your surgeon can help you calm these fears, not only with his explanations, but also by putting you in contact with others who have had the same operation you plan to have. Oftentimes it is easier to ask the difficult questions of a fellow patient who has been through surgery than it is to ask the surgeon.

If this appeals to you, ask the surgeon if he would put you in touch with another of his patients who has undergone the same operation you plan to have. The surgeon will first have to obtain the patient's consent to give you his or her name since not to do so would violate physician-patient confidentiality. The doctor should also give his other patient your name and explain why you will be calling.

Others who have been through the same surgery are a great resource for you and can be tremendously helpful in answering your questions and calming your fears. Should your surgeon not have anyone you can talk to, there are organizations of patients who work with patients undergoing surgery. For instance, Mended Hearts is a national organization of patients who have undergone heart operations, dedicated to helping those about to have such surgery. You will find a listing of such groups in Part V, "Resources."

I have discussed mutual respect as the basis of a sound relationship between you and your surgeon. Successful surgery requires another type of respect as well—respect for yourself. Remember, you are not a passive player in your operation, not a "slab of meat," as I have heard patients refer to themselves. You are an intelligent, active contributor to your operation. What you learn from this book, from your reading, from your doctors, and from other patients will help you to achieve successful surgery. You will have the power and strength that come from knowledge. You will have a strengthened mind-body connection. You will have self-confidence and self-respect. And with all of those, you can face anything.

The Hospital: No Place to Be Sick

You're going to need that self-respect to help you get through being in the hospital. Many people find hospitalization to be one of the most trying, humiliating experiences of their lives.

Unless you have a private room with armed guards, your privacy is shot to hell. Strangers—nurses, aides, technicians, residents, interns, housekeepers, television rental guys—walk into your room any time of day or night, usually without knocking. Most of those strangers can take a look at your naked or semi-clad body any old time they want to. (Presumably not the TV rental guy.) The clothing the hospital gives you to wear is usually a flimsy gown that is open at the back, giving you the opportunity to parade around the corridors with your butt hanging out.

You will be told what to eat and when. Someone will probably have to assist you to go to the bathroom. You will have needles, thermometers, and catheters inserted into various places in your body. The person in the bed next to you will snore loudly or play his TV all night long. He will have dozens of visitors who drop in just as you are falling asleep. You will discover the secret hospital regulation that requires your doctor to visit you only if you are eating, sleeping, visiting with your family, or going to the bathroom.

Joking aside, what may distress you the most about being in the hospital is the seeming indifference of the staff to your plight. The most common complaints I hear from my hospitalized patients stem from this. They feel that they must wait an interminable amount of time before a nurse answers a call bell. Or a nurse will promise to be right back and then never return. Or the patient can't obtain an extra blanket or get soiled bed linens changed.

The reason is not that nurses are thoughtless, insensitive people. Most of them go into nursing because they enjoy the opportunity to interact with people and help them. The problems are twofold. First, nurses are overworked and have so many responsibilities aside from direct patient care that they often do not have the time to give the nursing care they want to. Aside from helping you, they must distribute and keep track of medications, take and record vital signs, write reports in hospital charts, assist elderly and debilitated patients who are unable to care for themselves, and perform any other task no one else wants to do.

More often than not, there are insufficient nurses to handle the hospital's patient load. One nurse may be assigned to take care of several patients, one or two of whom are so sick that they consume most of the nurse's time. This is why I rarely hear complaints about the nursing in the intensive care units. There, each nurse is responsible for only a few patients and can concentrate her efforts on them.

The second problem that stands in the way of the personalized hospital care you might desire is human nature. To you, your hospital experience is unique, and you understandably want everything possible done to assist you. For many of the hospital staff, you are just one more person having surgery. I in no way intend this as criticism; it's a simple fact of life in any occupation. The routine becomes routine.

One more person's discomfort becomes no different from any other's. A patient's need to urinate is just one of many needs to urinate. Therefore, administering pain medication or helping someone to the bathroom become just one more task to be accomplished. A nurse or aide's personal sense of urgency is easily lost.

Further complicating this problem is the hospital staff's need to set priorities. The sickest people, those most in need, get helped first. You'll find that immediately after surgery you will get all the nursing attention you require. The problems come a few days later, when you are making a good recovery. By then, additional patients on the ward have just had surgery, and their needs will simply come before yours. That doesn't make you have to go to the bathroom any less, but helping you to do so will necessarily be a lower priority.

GETTING THE HOSPITAL STAFF ON YOUR SIDE

When I was growing up, my mother would quote two maxims her mother followed to get other people to do things. One was, "The squeaking wheel gets oiled," and the other was, "You catch more flies with honey than vinegar." I never figured out how Mom decided which strategy to employ in a given situation. I guess it depended on the mood she was in at the moment. Surely, either tactic would work in the hospital; I suggest you try the honey approach.

The way to get the best possible care from the hospital staff is to make yourself unique in their eyes. You don't want to be just one more "gall bladder" or "open heart" or "hip replacement." You want the staff to see you as a nice person whom it is a pleasure to take care of and whom they *want* to help. This is the key. The staff *have* to take care of the patients to whom they are assigned; it's their job. Your goal is to get them to *want* to care for you. Here's how:

- Show your appreciation from the moment you enter the hospital to the moment you leave. Sure, it's their job to help you, but everyone likes to feel that their efforts are appreciated. Express your gratitude to them.

- Bring a gift for the staff when you enter the hospital. As I said earlier, many people leave the nurses a box of chocolates when they depart the hospital. A nice gesture, but why not show your appreciation right from the start?

  It doesn't have to be anything elaborate. A small plant to put at the nursing station. (Not flowers; they get everyone's leftovers.) If you are handy with crafts, you might make something for them. Other ideas might be a book of inspirational sayings or of amusing cartoons. Even a greeting card thanking them in advance for their help will catch everyone's attention.

• Have family and friends around to help you. They can take up some slack for the nurses and will be particularly helpful around mealtimes. (Not surprisingly, studies have shown that patients with good social support recover better from illness than those who are alone.)

   I once worked in a tiny mountain hospital in rural Guatemala where the families lived, even cooked, right in the rooms with the patients. Patients benefited wonderfully from having their loved ones around twenty-four hours a day. Unfortunately, your family will have to respect the hospital's visiting hours. Also, the hospital administration will probably frown on a campfire in the room.

• Be as self-sufficient as possible. If the staff recognizes that you do as much for yourself as you can, they will know that if you ask for help, you need it. Some patients seem to regard the nurses as their personal servants, to be at their beck and call. This quickly becomes tiresome to even the most dedicated nursing professional, and you can be sure that her response time lengthens accordingly.

   Doing as much for yourself as you can will have the further benefit of speeding your recovery from surgery and getting you out of the hospital's clutches as quickly as possible.

• Let your demands equal your needs. As noted above, you will need more help right after surgery than you will a few days later. So don't expect the nurses to do as much for you later as they did earlier on. Also, try to anticipate your needs. If you wait until the last minute to ask for help to the bathroom, you are much more likely to find the wait excruciating. Remember that in the hospital things take time.

• Never forget that your nurse has other patients who need her as well. Showing consideration for others will earn you the same consideration for yourself.

• When all else fails, be a squeaky wheel.

CHAPTER CHECKLIST

Your Surgeon

☐ Go to the library and read about your operation.

☐ Prepare a list of questions for your surgeon.

☐ Research your surgeon's credentials.

☐ Be sure you give *informed* consent.

☐ Ask your surgeon about his experience with your particular operation.

☐ Request permission to contact another patient who has had similar surgery.

☐ Contact a patient support group (see "Resources," Part V).

The Hospital

☐ Obtain a small gift or card for the hospital staff.

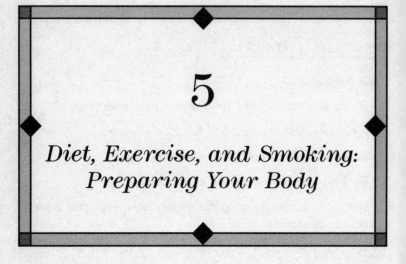

5

Diet, Exercise, and Smoking: Preparing Your Body

Mens sana in corpore sano.
(A sound mind in a sound body.)

—*Juvenal*

They that will not be counseled, cannot be helped. If you do
not hear reason, she will rap you on the knuckles.
—*Benjamin Franklin*

The only way to keep your health is to eat what you don't
want to, drink what you don't like, and do what you'd rather
not.

—*Mark Twain*

I could end this chapter right here. These sages have pretty
much told you everything about diet and exercise you need
to know. But I guess I should fill in the details.

We have spent a good deal of time discussing preparing
your mind for surgery, and you've already started by practic-

ing your self-relaxation exercises. *(You have, haven't you?)* So now let's spend a little time discussing how to prepare your body.

Could you imagine an athlete competing in a marathon without training properly? Of course not. A world-class marathoner runs more than twenty-six consecutive five-minute miles. That's an unbelievable pace, especially when you consider that the fastest milers are only about one minute and ten seconds faster for a single mile!

The stress on a marathoner's body is remarkable, and he or she wouldn't dream of competing without proper preparation. This includes eating the right foods and training extensively to strengthen muscles, heart, and lungs.

Of course, you may never run a marathon, but it is certainly true that the better condition you are in, the better prepared you will be to handle the physical stress of surgery.

Current circumstances may not allow you much preparation time, but even if time is short, starting now to eat properly and exercise your heart, lungs, and muscles will be helpful.

THE MoFoH PRINCIPLE

Getting started with a proper diet and regular exercise is difficult. Sticking with them is even harder. Changing habits is the most difficult thing I ever ask my patients to do.

I see this all the time in people with hypertension, or high blood pressure. Study after study has shown that lowering elevated blood pressure lowers the risk of heart attack, stroke, and kidney damage. I explain to patients that oftentimes reducing the salt in their diets, losing weight, and exercising moderately will help to get their pressures down, and they understand this. Almost all say they would prefer to try those steps before resorting to drugs.

Unfortunately, most of them eventually end up on medication. Sometimes this is because the above measures simply aren't effective for everyone. But more often than not, weight loss and exercise don't work because they're never really tried. Popping a pill is easy; changing how you live is hard.

It requires a great deal of self-motivation to break old habits and form new ones. Sometimes the motivation does not come until a person is lying on his back staring at the ceiling in the Intensive Care Unit. By then, it's a little late. Frankly, I think the **Mo**tivation that you have—upcoming surgery—is a great reason to start living more healthily.

(Now you're starting to see the emergence of the MoFoH principle. The term was inspired by magicians Penn & Teller, who perform a routine called "Mofo, the Psychic Gorilla.")

However, breaking old habits is tough. You simply have to make up your mind to **Fo**rce yourself to change. You need to remind yourself over and over why you must forego a rich dessert or head out and take a brisk walk when the cake and the couch seem so inviting. Each time you make yourself do something, it makes the next time a bit easier. And that time makes the next one easier, and so on until the new behavior becomes a **H**abit. And that's MoFoH: **Mo**tivation→**Fo**rced action→**H**abit.

Diet and Nutrition: Garbage In, Garbage Out

What applies to computers applies to our bodies. It doesn't matter how good a computer program is, if the data fed in are lousy, the results of all the millions of calculations the computer makes will also be lousy. The same goes for our bodies. They are wonderful mechanisms, but if we fuel them with garbage, they will perform poorly. You can help your body to withstand the stress of surgery by not feeding it garbage.

There's a lot of garbage in the field of nutrition, and I'm not referring simply to unhealthy foods. There are endless numbers of self-styled "nutritionists" ever ready to give you, or more often sell you, advice on what you should or should not eat. They range in innocence from your grandmother and her rules ("feed a cold, starve a fever") to calculating entrepreneurs who use scientific-sounding misinformation to sell their vitamins and other products.

Some promise to make you "fit for life," others to boost your immune system or your mental capacity. Still others try to convince you that all your ills result from food allergies, which their books tell you how to cure.

What follows in this chapter is sound, well-established dietary advice to guide you in the selection of foods to help your wonderful machine perform at its best and be ready for your operation.

SO WHAT WOULD BE A GOOD DIET FOR ME, ANYWAY?

I'm not going to tell you; I don't know you well enough. I don't know if you're thin or heavy, tall or short. I have no idea if you exercise regularly or sit around all the time. I haven't the foggiest notion where you eat your meals or who prepares them. I haven't got a clue about your medical history, your likes and dislikes, or which foods do or do not agree with you. In short, it would be silly for me to try to tell you precisely what to eat.

Since authors don't personally know their readers, it makes me chortle when I see a book with detailed dietary suggestions. Remember, we all have two eyes, a nose, and a mouth, but we all look different. Similarly, we all have stomachs, intestines, livers, and so on, and we are as different on the inside as we are on the outside. Only you can judge which foods are right for you, and nobody else can tell you exactly what to eat. The best I can do is give you guidelines to assist you in making your food selections.

A *Very Brief* Nutrition Course

Any diet has six basic components—carbohydrates, fats, proteins, water, vitamins, and minerals. What makes a diet good or bad is the relative proportions of these components. You've probably heard that most Americans have a poor diet: too much fat (correct); too few carbohydrates (correct again); overemphasis on protein (right); not enough vitamins (wrong).

There's a lot of nutritional information floating around out there, and for you to make intelligent food choices, you need to understand the six components and the roles they play in our health.

Carbohydrates include sugars, starches, and fiber. They are all made up of only two things, carbon and water. Actually, you already knew this. Remember what happened when, as a kid, your sugary campfire marshmallow caught on fire? You were left with black, disgusting stuff (the carbon) with steam coming off (the water).

Sugars are simple combinations of carbon and water and, not surprisingly, are called simple carbohydrates. *Starches* consist of many sugars linked together and consequently are referred to as complex carbohyrates. Isn't science wonderful?

The term *fiber* refers to a group of extremely complex carbohydrates that come from plants. Fiber passes through your body undigested. As you have no doubt heard, fiber helps our bodies to regulate our bowel movements. It may also play a role in reducing the risks of colon cancer and heart disease. Good stuff.

Carbohydrates come primarily from plants, so fruits and vegetables as well as foods made from plants (bread and pasta) are all excellent sources of both simple and complex carbohydrates.

These sugars and starches are our bodies' preferred energy

sources, and your diet should emphasize them. This may surprise you because somewhere along the line, carbohydrates have picked up a reputation for being fattening. This is wrong, but haven't we all seen someone on a diet order a hamburger, discard the bread and eat the meat? Actually, he or she should be doing just the opposite. Our bodies use carbohydrates very efficiently, and unless we eat huge amounts of them, very little is actually turned into fat. Since bread is high in carbohydrates, you'd have to eat a lot more than a single bun to worry about gaining weight from it.

The hamburger, however, is very high in **fat** and, therefore, is much more fattening. (Isn't language wonderful?) Fats come from both plant and animal foods, but with a few exceptions, the nasty ones come primarily from animal sources.

Even though fats do deserve much of the bad reputation they've acquired, they are an essential part of our diets, and we could not live without eating some. Also, without fats, foods would be less enjoyable. It is fats that give foods a full, satisfying feeling in the mouth. In fact, when people think they have a *sweet* tooth, what they really have is a *fat* tooth. What they crave is not the sweetness of the sugar, but the texture of the fat; that's why they find a slice of cake to be more gratifying than a piece of fruit.

The problem with fats is that they contribute to heart disease and some forms of cancer, and we consume too much of them. About half the calories in the average American diet come from fat. It should be down below thirty percent.

Fortunately, it is now easier than ever to determine the fat contents of foods we buy. A fat-healthy food is one that derives fewer than twenty percent of its calories from fat. The "Nutrition Facts" labels on foods make it easy to determine if a food you buy is fat-healthy.

For instance, here are the labels from two brands of crackers I found on the shelf of our pantry. First, here is a very popular cracker:

Nutrition Facts

Serving Size 5 Crackers (16g)
Servings Per Container About 21

Amount Per Serving

Calories 80	Calories from Fat 35
	% Daily Value

Total Fat 4g	**6%**
Saturated Fat	**4%**
Polyunsaturated Fat 0g	
Monounsaturated Fat 1.5g	
Cholesterol 0mg	**0%**
Sodium 135mg	**6%**
Total Carbohydrate 10g	**3%**
Dietary Fiber Less than 1 gram	**1%**
Sugars 1g	
Protein 1g	

Look at the top of the label where it says "Amount Per Serving." You'll see that one serving of these crackers has eighty calories. Right next to that the label informs you that thirty-five of those calories derive from fat. Well, thirty-five is a little less than half of eighty, so you can see that almost fifty percent of this cracker's calories are fat calories. Here is a label from a "reduced fat" cracker made by the same company:

Nutrition Facts

Serving Size 32 Crackers (30g)
Servings Per Container About 5

Amount Per Serving

Calories 120	Calories from Fat 15
	% Daily Value

Total Fat 2g	**3%**
Saturated Fat	**0%**
Polyunsaturated Fat 0g	
Monounsaturated Fat 0.5g	
Cholesterol 0mg	**0%**
Sodium 290mg	**12%**
Total Carbohydrate 23g	**8%**
Dietary Fiber 1 gram	**3%**
Sugars 2g	
Protein 2g	

Here, only fifteen of each serving's 120 calories, or about twelve and a half percent, come from fat. This snack cracker is not just "reduced fat," but also "reduced guilt."

A huge variety of **proteins** are found throughout our tissues and organs and serve innumerable functions. All proteins are made of twenty-two building blocks called *amino acids*. When we eat proteins, digestion breaks them down into their component amino acids. The amino acids travel through the blood to all the various cells of the body, where the amino acids are reassembled into the proteins that any given cell needs.

We do not have to eat large amounts of protein to meet the body's requirements. In fact, the body can even break down amino acids we have eaten and reform them into most of the amino acids it needs. Any extra protein consumed is converted to the sugar glucose and burned for energy or stored as fat.

Plants, especially legumes, grains, and nuts, are excellent sources of protein. So are meat and dairy products, though these foods carry the burden of high fat content. If you plan to get most of your dietary protein from plant foods, be sure to eat a wide variety of them so that you will get everything you need, including the so-called *essential amino acids* your body cannot manufacture on its own.

We don't often think of the importance of **water** in our diets until we go for a while without it. Then our thirst reminds us. Water is the most plentiful and hardest-working substance in us. It accounts for about fifty-five to seventy percent of our adult weight and also serves to transport nutrients, keep us cool, and excrete wastes. It is a part of many of the chemical reactions that are constantly going on inside us.

You might be surprised that most adults consume about one and a half to three quarts of water per day. A significant portion of this water comes from our food, not necessarily from what we actually drink. We also lose a lot of water each day, not only through urination and perspiration, which we are aware of, but also via so-called insensible loss through our breath and skin.

The Vitamin Myth

I am always astonished by the reverence with which people regard **vitamins.** These common nutrients have acquired the reputation of being able to promote growth, boost energy, protect the body against stress, prevent some illnesses, vanquish others, prolong life, and enhance sexual performance. What more could any red-blooded American want?

Too bad most of it's not true.

The fact is that while preparing for surgery you do not need to take any vitamin supplements beyond what your surgeon might recommend.

Vitamins derive their name from two words, *vital* and *amines*. Literally, they are substances that are essential for many of the chemical reactions that take place in our bodies. What characterizes a vitamin is that a deficiency of it produces a particular disease state. For instance, a deficiency of vitamin C causes scurvy, in which there is a breakdown of skin and other tissues. If you lack vitamin B_{12}, you will suffer from anemia and neurological disorders. For every vitamin, there is a specific deficiency disease that is remedied by restoring that vitamin to the body.

However, some of today's supposed vitamin deficiency conditions are based more on marketing studies than scientific fact. For instance, many vitamin companies market "stress formulas" that contain large doses of niacin and the B vitamins—B_1, B_2, B_6, and B_{12}. The companies claim that stress depletes these vitamins from our bodies and leaves us lacking energy.

As is often the case with modern myths, there is a modicum of truth as the basis of this claim. Vitamins B_1, B_2, and niacin assist in the biochemical processes that enable the individual cells in our bodies to extract energy from food. It *almost* seems logical that since these vitamins are needed by the body to produce energy, if you're lacking energy, you should take these vitamins to restore it.

But almost isn't good enough; this thinking represents a great leap of logic from known facts to false conclusions. There is no evidence whatsoever that people who are fatigued from stress are deficient in any of the B vitamins or niacin. In the case of B_{12}, it takes a lot more than stress to deplete the body's huge stored supply of this vitamin.

What's important to remember about vitamins is that we require only small amounts of them to remain healthy. There seems to be, however, a part of the modern psyche that presumes that if some is good, more must be better, and a lot must be great! Yet, there is little evidence that taking more vitamins than you can obtain by eating healthfully provides any health benefit at all.* This is not something the U.S.'s $3 billion-a-year vitamin industry wants you to know.

Finally we come to another small but crucial component of our healthy diets, **minerals.** These are inorganic (that is, not derived from living sources) elements that play important roles in many body functions. Some minerals, such as calcium and phosphorus, the major components of bones, are found in relatively large amounts in our bodies. Similarly, sodium and potassium, which perform many functions, from enabling our nerves to work to helping to regulate our body fluids, are also plentiful. These minerals, as well as magnesium, sulfur, and chloride, fall into the category of *macro*minerals, because we have a lot of them.

The other category is *micro*minerals, substances of which our bodies have only trace amounts. Some of these are copper, zinc, and selenium.

*Even the studies showing some benefit from taking antioxidant vitamins—C, E, and beta-carotene—are preliminary and need to be confirmed with further research.

As with vitamins, deficiencies of individual minerals are associated with particular disease states. Iron deficiency causes anemia. Insufficient calcium causes osteoporosis, or brittle bones, in adults. If we lose excessive amounts of potassium, because of diarrhea or diuretic ("water pill") medications, muscle cramps and irregular heartbeats can result.

The roles of some of the microminerals are less well understood. We know, for instance, that a lack of zinc can cause delayed wound healing. (For this reason, your surgeon may prescribe zinc supplements to you before your operation.) We also know that selenium works with vitamin E to prevent the breakdown of certain body chemicals, but no studies have shown what happens if the diet is deficient in selenium. This is because we need such tiny amounts of it that, short of severe starvation, it is very hard to develop a selenium deficiency.

The gaps in our knowledge have not, however, prevented clever marketers from selling mineral supplements supposedly to promote better health. With the exceptions of pregnancy, lactation, calcium to prevent osteoporosis, and certain other medical conditions, there is rarely reason to take mineral supplements. These substances are so ubiquitous in our diets that rational eating habits, even fairly irrational eating habits, provide all the minerals we need.

Dr. Bob's Presurgical Diet

Eating should be enjoyable. One way sure to make it less so is to burden yourself with too many rules and calculations. A lot of health books have you adding up calories, figuring the percentages derived from fat and protein, and measuring portions. What a bore! Besides, who's got time to do that?

My dietary advice is based on the most recent U.S. Department of Agriculture guidelines. It is sensible, easy to follow, and tasty. Yes, you may have to eat less of certain foods that have been staples of your current diet, but, interestingly enough, human beings have been known to survive without potato chips.

Eating this way will enable your body to perform at its best when faced with the stress of surgery.

WHAT TO EAT

As promised, I'm not going to burden you with a lot of strict rules. So let me pass on to you the best nutritional advice I have encountered. The editors of the *Tufts University Diet and Nutrition Letter* summarized the essence of a healthful diet in nine words: more plant foods, fewer animal foods, and more exercise. We'll get to exercise later in this chapter; for now let's concentrate on foods.

More Plant Foods

The mainstay of a healthy diet is complex carbohydrates, the starches found in a great variety of fruits, vegetables, grains, nuts, and beans. Most of the calories* in our diets should come from these sources. Carbohydrates contain less than half the calories of a similar amount of fat, and our bodies digest and burn the calories from carbohydrates very efficiently.

Carbohydrates have another major advantage. Because they derive from plant sources, they come prepackaged with lots of vitamins and minerals and some protein to boot. And as an added bonus, the packaging is also high in dietary fiber.

In building a diet around complex carbohydrates, be sure to choose a variety of foods you enjoy. There are plenty of carbohydrate-rich foods out there to select from. **Pasta** and **whole-grain breads** are a good starting place. Remember, de-

---

*A *calorie* is a measure of an amount of energy, just as a *watt* is a measure of energy put out by a lightbulb. In our bodies, calories are released by the foods we eat. A food with more calories provides more energy, but if we consume more calories than we use, we store the extra energy in the form of fat.

spite what you may have grown up thinking, these are not fattening foods. The problem comes with what you put on them. Bread is great until you load on the butter, and noodles are fine unless they are buried under beef goulash. So, use a thin layer of soft margarine on that bread and tomato sauce on those noodles, and you'll be fine.

Be careful about commercially baked goods, especially cakes, cookies, muffins, and biscuits. They are usually quite high in fat, particularly saturated fat. Generally, hard rolls, English muffins, pita breads and crusty French or Italian breads are good choices. Many supposedly healthful bran muffins are nothing of the sort. The bran they contain is offset by their large amount of fat.

Another good carbohydrate food is **cereal,** provided you're not thinking about those super-sweet cartoon-character concoctions aimed at kids. Particularly good are the raisin brans, the multigrain cereals, and good old-fashioned oatmeal (though the "instant" variety has lost some of its vitamins). Avoid any cereal where sugar or corn sweetener is the first or second ingredient listed. Also, don't be overly impressed by cereals promising to provide one hundred percent of the recommended daily allowances of vitamins. There is no law of nutrition that says you have to get a whole day's worth of vitamins in one meal.

When it comes to nutrition, **potatoes** are no small potatoes. They are high in nutrients and fiber and low in calories. The problem is that they are not especially palatable raw, so human beings have devised a number of ways to ruin potatoes nutritionally through cooking and seasoning them unwisely. Most destructive is deep frying, which both destroys vitamins and boosts calories. Also, it shoots fat content into the stratosphere. Boil, steam, or bake your potatoes. Go *very* easy with the margarine, and get that sour cream and au-gratin stuff the heck out of there.

A billion people can't all be wrong; about one third of the

world's population uses **rice** as the mainstay of their diets. We would be well off to follow their lead. Brown rice is the healthiest choice, but "converted" rice also retains many nutrients. As with potatoes, be careful what you put on rice. My wife's Greek family seasons it with fresh lemon juice rather than butter, an idea that shocked me until I found out how good it is.

Ever wonder what those highly touted **legumes** are? They're beans, from kidney to lima to soy to pinto. They are pretty good sources of carbohydrates, and they are also rich in proteins. This is especially important if your protein intake is reduced because you are cutting down on animal foods. Legumes and **nuts** also provide lots of vitamins and minerals. Go easy on the nuts, though, since they are high in fat.

Your mother always insisted you eat your **vegetables,** and she was right. They have plenty of vitamins and minerals as well as fiber. The same goes for **fruits.** If you can, try to have fresh fruits and vegetables that have been harvested locally. The ones that have been picked early and ripened off the tree or vine are less nutritious.

I must caution you that eating a high-carbohydrate diet may come with a price. One of the main by-products of starch and fiber digestion is intestinal gas. And I don't mean burping. You can reduce the chance of having excessive intestinal gas by starting on a high-carbohydrate diet gradually and building up. Oftentimes, gassiness resolves after a few embarrassing days.

Fewer Animal Foods

Please note that the operative word is *fewer,* not *no*. In addition to their taste, there are too many good things about meat, poultry, fish, and dairy products simply to dump them from our diets. They are good sources of protein—including the essential amino acids our bodies cannot make—vitamins, and minerals. Also, they add considerable variety to what we eat. The problem is that most animal products have a lot of fat, and most of that is saturated fat, the one that helps clog up arteries. Therefore, it is important to choose animal foods carefully to limit the amount of saturated fat you consume.

Red meats (beef, pork, veal, ham, lamb) are particularly high in saturated fats, and you should limit them significantly. When you do eat them, avoid "prime cuts," which are heavily marbled with fat, and trim off any visible fat. Processed meats such as salami and baloney are *extremely* high in fat. "Lean" is preferable to regular hamburger meat.

Incidentally, food scientists at the University of Minnesota have found a way to cook ground meat that reduces its fat content from twenty-seven percent to seven percent. First, brown the meat in a nonstick pan and pour off the fat. Then, rinse the meat with hot water and drain again. It's as simple as that. When the fat is removed, you lose some of the flavor, and the meat does not hold together as well. Still, this is a great way to make meat more healthful for chili, spaghetti sauces, and other dishes where you use ground beef.

Instead of red meat, try substituting **fish** and white-meat **chicken** and **turkey**, since they all contain less saturated fat. Remove the skin from poultry before or after cooking it, and you'll avoid eating two-thirds of the fat. Also, you'll be better off broiling, baking, steaming, or poaching these foods, rather than sautéing or deep frying them.

Shellfish are another substitute for red meat. Although they are actually high in cholesterol, they do not affect the amount of cholesterol in your blood because they are very low in saturated fats. Also, they contain a kind of fat called omega-3 polyunsaturates, which may have a protective effect against coronary artery disease.

Choose your **milk** and **dairy** products carefully. Milk should be low-fat—skimmed or one percent fat. (Whole milk contains four percent fat.) Hard cheeses tend to be very high in fat, especially the saturated variety. Rich, creamy products such as cream, ice cream, frozen custard (also called soft-serve ice cream), and sour cream should be rare treats. Fortunately, manufacturers are responding to consumers' desires for low-fat dairy products with a variety of products, including low-fat frozen yogurts, part-skim-milk cheeses, and cheese substitutes.

Oils

The goal of reducing the amount of animal food we eat is to reduce the amount of fat in our diets. Of course, getting some fat is unavoidable, and even essential. However, by choosing vegetable sources of fat for your diet, you can see to it that you consume more of the more healthful polyunsaturated and monounsaturated varieties.

Major dietary sources of polyunsaturated fats are liquid **vegetable oils**—corn, safflower, sunflower, cottonseed, soybean, and canola. A popular oil these days is olive, which is high in monounsaturated fats. Recent research has shown that people for whom olive oil is a major source of fat calories have lower incidences of cardiac disease. Consequently, there is a lot of research going on to determine if olive oil is actually good for you (a question Popeye answered years ago).

You will increase your intake of the good fats by using soft margarine rather than butter or stick margarine. In margarine, the oil is "partially hydrogenated" to make it hard. What this does is convert some of the polyunsaturated fat to saturated fat, just what we don't want. Look for a soft margarine with polyunsaturated to saturated fat ratio of at least two to one.

Tropical oils (coconut, palm, cocoa butter) are among the few vegetable derivatives that contain high concentrations of saturated fats. Also, painful as it is for me to say, chocolate is very high in saturated vegetable fat, and you should limit the amount you eat.

Tropical oils and hydrogenated vegetable oils are commonly used as additives in nondairy milk or cream substitutes and in many commercially prepared bakery products, candies, and fried foods. It is important to read labels, as I discussed earlier. Such products may be advertised as "cholesterol-free," which is technically correct. However, these foods' high saturated-fat content makes them unhealthful.

PUTTING IT ALL TOGETHER

I've given you a lot of information, but what I haven't done is give you an actual diet to follow. As I said at the beginning, I can't. Also, I don't think you want to spend your time counting calories, calculating percentages from fat and protein, counting servings, and measuring portion sizes. However, to show you that eating properly really is easy and tasty, I've put together two days' worth of healthful menus that incorporate the principles I've set out. As a special bonus, I've also given you a selection of not-so-bad snacks to choose from.

DAY 1

BREAKFAST
Orange juice
Bagel or toast with jam or small amount of margarine
Decaf coffee or tea with low-fat milk

LUNCH
Cold pasta and vegetable salad
Whole-grain bread thinly spread with margarine
Piece of fruit

DINNER
Tossed salad with olive oil and vinegar
Broiled skinless chicken breast
Baked potato

Green vegetable of choice
Roll and margarine
Low-fat frozen yogurt
Water

DAY 2

BREAKFAST

Half a grapefruit
Raisin bran cereal with low-fat milk and a banana
Decaf coffee or tea

LUNCH

Tuna sandwich using low-fat mayo on whole wheat with lettuce
and tomato
Pretzels
Cup of low-fat yogurt
Seltzer or diet soda

DINNER

Mixed salad
Spaghetti with meat sauce (drain fat from meat as described above)
Parmesan cheese (sprinkled lightly)
Italian bread with margarine
Chocolate cake (occasionally acceptable irrational choice)

Not so bad, is it? These two days emphasize breads and
cereals, fruits and vegetables, while limiting protein and animal fat. Also, the foods here provide all the vitamins and
minerals you need without taking supplements.

About those snacks. Aside from the obviously healthful
ones such as fruit, some seemingly "bad" things are actually
okay. Pretzels, for instance, are baked, not fried, and thus are
generally low in fat. You might want to buy the salt-free ones,
though. Popcorn, especially when air popped, is also a healthful snack. Don't blow it with butter, though. Some cookies,

such as vanilla wafers, gingersnaps, graham crackers, and fig bars, are relatively low in fat. Also, fat-free baked products are proliferating in markets. (Remember, though, that although these are low in fat, they are not necessarily low in calories.) Low- and no-fat frozen yogurts are good substitutes for ice cream. There is even one candy bar that is less noxious than the others. Three Musketeers actually has less saturated fat than most, so if you're really desperate for candy, there's one you can choose with a minimum of guilt.

Having said that, I would like to comment briefly on **sugar** in the diet. Sugar has acquired a really bad reputation, some of it deserved. It certainly does promote tooth decay. And many products with sugar or other sweeteners in them contain lots of calories with little nutritional value—soda, for instance. Sugar does not cause some of the bad things attributed to it, though. For instance, eating too much sugar will not make you diabetic. If you do eat excess sugar, you could end up being too fat, and that can lead to diabetes, but not the sugar itself. Also, there is no good scientific evidence that sugar consumption in children causes hyperactivity, despite what some popular books would have you believe.

Nevertheless, because sugar and sweeteners add little to your diet other than calories, you should try to limit the amount you consume.

Another thing to limit is **salt.** Remember that salt is sodium chloride, a sodium atom hooked to a chlorine atom. The sodium is the problem with salt. While the average person can consume a large amount of sodium without too much harm, there is no doubt that our diets provide far more of this mineral than we actually need. Also, for some people, sodium may be a contributing factor to the development of hypertension, or high blood pressure.

Americans consume about fifteen pounds of salt a year each. Many of us are very liberal with the saltshaker. On top of that, salt is the most common additive in commercially prepared foods. Sodium is particularly plentiful in canned vegetables and fish, processed meats and cheeses, and commercial cereals and breads, even when these foods don't taste especially salty.

Every dietary authority recommends limiting salt in the diet, and this is really quite easy to do. You see, salt is an acquired taste, and you can unacquire it. I suggest you do this in stages. First, eliminate highly salted foods from your diet. This includes not only blatantly salty things such as potato chips and pickles, but also those foods noted above in which the salt is not so obvious.

Next, get the saltshaker off the table. Many people reach for it even before they taste their food. That's silly. If you stop automatically salting your food, you may find at first that the food seems to taste a bit bland. I promise you that after a short while you won't miss the salt. Food tastes fine without it.

The next step is not to add salt when cooking. Again, you may initially notice a different taste to your food. You might want to make up for a salt with herbs and spices, pepper, garlic powder (*not* garlic salt), onion powder, or lemon juice.

I have followed this regimen myself. At first, it was difficult, but I rapidly lost my taste for salt. The proof came one day when someone offered me a salty pretzel, previously my favorite snack, and I was unable to eat it. It tasted much too salty!

BAD TO THE LAST DROP

Quick. What is the most widely used addictive drug in the United States?

Cocaine? Nope.

Heroin? Guess again.

Nicotine? Close, but no cigar.

The answer is coffee. The average American consumes eight hundred cups of brew a year. In fact, half of all the coffee in the world is drunk right here. Yet, this seemingly innocuous drink, which is so enjoyed and savored by those handsome actors and actresses in coffee commercials is, in fact, an addicting stimulant drug.

But is caffeine really addicting? Well, if you are a coffee drinker, ask yourself these questions: Do you drink more coffee than you really want to? If you try to cut down on your coffee consumption, do you find yourself missing it? Do you continue to drink coffee, even though you suspect that it is having some adverse effects? Do you find that you need to drink more coffee to get the same effect (Gee, one cup just doesn't get me going like it used to)? If you suddenly cut out coffee, do you experience fatigue, headaches, nervousness, or even depression? And if you do get such withdrawal symptoms, does a cup of coffee make them go away?

You only have to answer *yes* to three of those questions to meet the official criteria for "psychoactive substance dependence," fancy terminology for addiction.

Eliminating coffee from your diet prior to surgery is important for two reasons. First is that you should not be using any drug that might in any way interfere with your surgery. Caffeine is a stimulant that can cause a rapid heartbeat, irritability, nervousness, anxiety, insomnia, and palpitations. Secondly, after your surgery you may not be able to eat or drink for a few days. If you are unknowingly addicted to caffeine, your recovery from surgery could be complicated by caffeine withdrawal symptoms such as headaches and irritability.

Caffeine is found not only in coffee. Caffeine is also in tea, cocoa, chocolate, cola beverages, some noncola soft drinks such as Mountain Dew and Dr Pepper, and many prescription and over-the-counter medications. Be especially on the lookout for caffeine in pain relievers and cold remedies. Read labels.

HOW TO DO IT

There are two schools of thought on how to cut caffeine intake. I call them the tough guys and the smart guys.

The tough guys say to stop drinking coffee cold turkey. Just quit it. Oh, yes, you'll probably get some headaches. You'll be irritable. You'll crave that java. But the experience of undergoing withdrawal symptoms will make you realize how addicted you were to coffee, and you'll feel that much better when all the effects wear off.

I think that's like banging your head against the wall because it feels so good when you stop.

The more sensible approach is a gradual withdrawal from caffeine. It takes a little more time, but you'll feel better during the process, and in the end you'll be just as free of caffeine as the person who quits cold turkey.

One way to eliminate caffeine is to mix regular and decaffeinated coffee together, gradually decreasing the amount of regular and increasing the proportion of decaf. I think this is cumbersome and difficult to keep track of. Instead, try cutting back by one cup of regular coffee every day.

Suppose you drink five cups of coffee a day. On the first day you start to cut down, have four cups of regular and one cup of instant decaffeinated. (This contains about two milligrams of caffeine, compared to about 140 for drip brewed.) The following day, have three cups of regular coffee and two of the decaf. On the third day, cut back to two regular cups and three decaf. Et cetera, et cetera.

Once you are having five cups of decaffeinated instant coffee per day, start eliminating one of those each day until you are down to none. If you miss having some form of hot liquid, try one of the commercial herbal teas available in supermarkets. I'd avoid the herbal teas found in so-called health food stores, as many of these concoctions contain substances as potentially harmful as coffee.

As you are eliminating caffeine, please keep in mind the other products beside coffee that contain it, as noted above.

And any time you feel you are missing something by not drinking coffee, remember that the man who measured out his life with coffee spoons was T. S. Eliot's J. Alfred Prufrock.

THE ALTERNATIVE DIET

A patient of mine, after learning that I was writing this book, gave me a copy of the following diet. Its authorship is unknown, and it was clearly a thirty-seventh generation photocopy. This diet is one of those bits of office wisdom that gains new adherents every time it is faxed somewhere new. Read and enjoy.

And eat at your own risk.

THIS DIET IS DESIGNED TO HELP YOU COPE WITH THE STRESS THAT BUILDS UP DURING THE DAY.

BREAKFAST
Half a grapefruit
One slice whole-wheat toast
Eight oz. skim milk

LUNCH
Four-oz. broiled skinless chicken breast
One cup steamed spinach
One cup herbal tea
One chocolate chip cookie

AFTERNOON SNACK
Remainder of cookies in package

DINNER
One loaf garlic bread with cheese
One large pepperoni & onion pizza
Four cans or one pitcher of beer
One pint Rocky Road ice cream
Toppings of choice

LATE-NIGHT SNACK

Entire frozen cheesecake eaten directly from freezer

Exercise for People Who Hate to Exercise

If you already pursue a regular regimen of exercise, more power to you, but this part of the chapter is not for you. You already know the great benefits of being in good physical shape, and your conditioning will stand you in good stead for surgery. Skip to the next section, "Mind-Body Preparation Scripts," and I'll chat with these other folks.

Okay. Now that we've gotten rid of those self-righteous, goody-two-shoes health nuts, let me have a word with the rest of you, the committed nonexercisers. You are probably thinking, "What's the point? What can I do between now and surgery that can help me?" The answer is plenty. In fact, *anything* you do between now and the day of your operation will be helpful. The stronger your heart, lungs, and muscles the better.

I understand why up till now you've never exercised. First of all, you're probably too busy even to think about exercising; it does take up time. It also hurts while you're doing it. You smell afterward. As it is, you wake up early to go to work; how are you going to get up an hour earlier to jog in the darkness and risk getting hit by a car? And after the kind of days you put in, the last thing you want to do when you get home is put on sneakers and work up a sweat. Besides, you'll never look like those models in the ads because they have nothing better to do all day except work out in some gym and pose for pictures. Believe me, I understand how you feel.

I really don't want to convince you to exercise. But could we talk for a moment about walking?

Yes, walking. It's such a mundane, natural part of our lives that we hardly give it any thought. But walking is wonderful. Both research studies and real people have discovered that walking is a great stress reliever as well as a great way to build up your heart and lungs. One important reason for this is that walking comes so naturally to us. You don't have to concentrate as you do it; you just go. Some people consider swimming to be relaxing, but they have to think about what they're doing at least enough to keep from drowning. Other people talk about the runner's high they get from jogging; ask them about the runner's low they get from injuries. Bicycling is fine, but who wants to battle cars for a share of the roads or combat boredom on one of those stupid stationary bikes?

Taking a walk is easy. It doesn't take much time, and it gives you the opportunity to get away from everything and clear your head. Study after study has shown that walking does your heart and lungs almost as much good as jogging, with much less chance of injury. And with walking, you smell less.

One caution before you begin to exercise. If you are over thirty-five, have not exercised in ages, have heart problems, diabetes, high blood pressure, or another significant medical problem, or if you take medication regularly, **please consult your physician.** There may be certain precautions she will want you take.

Finally, if your medical condition prevents you from walking, there are other forms of exercise you can do. I'll describe these at the end of the chapter.

WALKING—THE FIRST STEPS

The hardest thing about starting to walk is *starting* to walk. It's simply a question of inertia. You are not used to doing it; so it probably seems like a great effort to get going. And in some sense it is. As Newton pointed out, a body at rest tends to stay at rest.

However, Sir Isaac also taught us that a body in motion tends to stay in motion. Walking is so enjoyable that once you start, you will really want to keep doing it. Also, as you discover how wonderful a good walk makes you feel, you will soon start to look forward to taking your next one.

Although he didn't know it, Sir Isaac was actually enunciating a variation of the MoFoH principle. Your **M**otivation to walk is your desire to be in the best condition possible for surgery. This is the power that overcomes your inertia. You have to **F**orce yourself to make the time to take those first few walks. Once you have done so, you will enjoy walking so much that **H**abit will keep your body in motion for a long time.

So, here's how to get started. First of all, you will need decent walking shoes. These certainly don't have to be space-age, high-tech, super-sole, air-power, pumped-up foot fashion statements. After all, purchasing sneakers should leave you with enough money for food and rent. However, the shoes you select should have two crucial features, support and comfort.

Most of the popular athletic shoes sold today provide good support, but before you agree to take anything home from the store, be sure they're very comfortable. Don't let the salesperson convince you they need breaking in. Try on different brands until you find a pair that feels just right. Nothing can kill your ambition to talk like two sore feet.

DAY 1

We all accomplish more if we are working toward a goal, so let me give you one. *Eventually,* I hope you will work up to the point where you will be walking for twenty to thirty continuous minutes at a comfortably brisk pace three or four times a week. Right now, that may seem like a pretty daunting task, sort of like dropping a copy of *Hamlet* in front of a first grader and promising, "Soon, you'll read this."

The key word is *eventually.* I don't know or even care how long it takes you to reach that goal. I don't even care *if* you reach this goal before your operation. I don't know at what level of fitness, or lack thereof, you're starting. You might be able to go out and take that walk right now. Well, go ahead! Or you may find that a ten-minute walk is your current limit. Fine! Two minutes of brisk strolling might be all you can muster. That's okay, too. All that matters is that you start.

But before you take that first step, it is important to warm up your muscles a little. You want to get the blood flowing in them before you start to work them. The best way to do this is to walk at a leisurely pace for about three minutes to get the circulation going and then do some simple, gentle stretching exercises.

Stretching is very important to get the muscles ready for more vigorous activity. If you don't stretch, you risk injuring muscles, even if you are only taking a brisk walk.

Here are four simple stretches to do *after* you have warmed up your muscles by walking casually for about three minutes.

Waist bends. Stand with your feet about shoulder width apart and put your hands on your hips. Slowly bend forward at the waist until your back really doesn't want you to go any farther. Then, allow your arms to dangle down naturally in front of you. You will feel a gentle tugging from your calves, up through the backs of your thighs, into your lower back, and up to your shoulders.

Now, just hold this position for a slow count of ten. *Don't bounce* down there. Just allow yourself to fold over gently and let the muscles loosen up in that bent-over position. Bouncing actually activates special nerve receptors in the muscles that cause the muscles to tighten, just the opposite of what you are trying to achieve.

After a count of ten, straighten up, replace your hands on your hips, and lean back a bit, arching your back. This time, you'll feel the pulling in the front of your thighs and your lower back. Don't overdo this one. If you hear popping and cracking in your back, you're doing too much. Once again, hold the position for a count of ten.

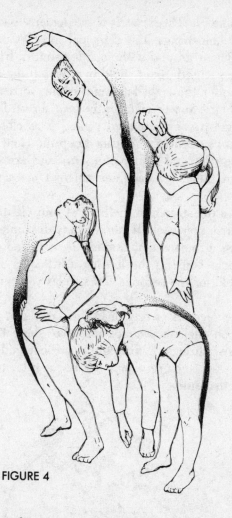

FIGURE 4

After straightening up, lean gently toward your right or left. The arm opposite the side you lean toward arches up over your head. The other hand stays on your hip. Hold this for ten more seconds and then lean over to the opposite side for ten seconds. Twice around these four positions will start to loosen the large muscles of your legs and back.

Thigh looseners. This stretch is particularly good for the buttocks and hamstrings, the principal muscles of walking. Sit on the floor or ground with your legs out in front of you with the knees slightly bent. Fold in your left leg so that its foot passes under the right knee and comes to rest beneath your right thigh. Slowly and gently lean forward and with both hands grasp your extended right leg as close to your right ankle as you comfortably can. Keep the right ankle anchored where it is, and gently pull with your arms, thereby stretching out the lower back and thigh. Once again, don't bounce.

You will feel the stretch in the back of your right thigh and a little in your upper back. If you feel any discomfort in your bent left knee, it means that the left leg is folded under the right too much. Unbend the left leg a little. As before, the position is held for ten seconds. Then relax your grip and sit back up.

After a few seconds of rest, lean forward again and grasp the ankle for another ten seconds and relax. Repeat one more time. Then switch legs, folding the right foot under the extended left leg and repeating three gentle ten-second stretches on that side.

FIGURE 5

Calf stretches. For your last loosening exercise, stand facing a wall an arm's length from it. If you reach out and put your palms flat on the wall, your body should be straight up, perpendicular to the floor, and your elbows should be straight. Keeping your heels flat on the floor, slowly bend your elbows and allow yourself to lean in toward the wall. Be sure to keep your heels flat on the ground. If you can, keep leaning in until your cheek touches the wall. At first, it may

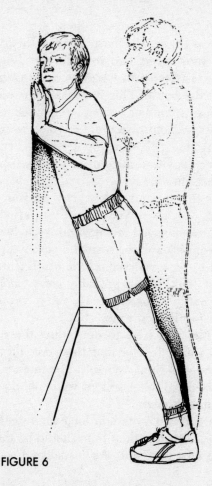

FIGURE 6

feel as if you are stretching the calves too much. In that case, first bend your head down and then lean in until your forehead touches the wall.

Once again, hold the position for ten seconds without bouncing. Then push yourself back to the upright position. Repeat twice with a few seconds' rest between stretches.

Now let's walk.

STEPPING OFF

There are three things you have to know before you set out: your route, your speed, and your duration. As silly as it may seem, I suggest you plan where you are going to walk before you leave the house. This is so that your walk will be automatic. Choose a familiar route. Remember, one of the things that makes walking pleasurable is not having to think about what you're doing. If you stop at every corner or fork in the road to decide where to go next, you lose some of that freedom from thought.

Walk at a pace that is comfortably brisk *for you*. It is not a casual stroll; that you do in your warm-up period. Nor are you trying to set a land speed record. I think the best description for the type of walk and the resultant pace is a purposeful stride. You want to push yourself *a little bit*. If you are out of breath after your walk, you've probably gone too fast. If you feel as if you've barely done anything, you've probably gone too slowly or for insufficient time.

As I said earlier, you have to determine the duration of your first walks yourself. The first time out, do what feels comfortable without pushing yourself. The moment you start to feel tired, slow down to a stroll for your cool-down period, as we'll discuss in a moment.

When you start to tire, note how long you've been walking at the brisk pace. That length of time should be the duration of your walk the next time out. For instance, if you find that after five minutes of brisk walking you are starting to feel as if you are pushing it, your subsequent walks should also be five minutes. After several days, you will notice that at the end of five minutes you don't really feel tired anymore. Congratulations! You have gotten yourself in better shape. On your next walk, try going for six or seven minutes. When that feels comfortable, try eight or ten minutes.

There is no shame in building up gradually. Don't be discouraged by a seeming lack of progress. As long as you push your body a little bit, it will respond to the challenge by growing stronger. And every little bit of conditioning will help you through surgery.

As I said at the outset, a reasonable goal is to walk for twenty to thirty minutes at a comfortably brisk pace without stopping. This duration was not chosen randomly. Studies have shown that the best results for cardiovascular fitness are achieved with at least twenty minutes of exercise. However, exercising for shorter periods of time is helpful, too, so any walking you do before surgery will be helpful.

Most people like to walk every other day, three to four times a week. If you want to walk every day, so much the better, but this is not absolutely necessary. Here are a few simple tips that will help keep your walking enjoyable:

If you can, try to walk at the same time every day. The specific time you choose is a matter of personal choice, though there are good reasons for particular times. If you walk first thing in the morning, you will feel energized for the rest of the day. Also, the air is often fresher in the early morning. Some people like to walk during their lunch breaks. This certainly saves calories, and it's a good way to relieve some of the morning's stress. For this reason, walking after work is also a good idea. You can relax after a tough day and probably be in a better mood for dinner.

Vary your route. Maybe you'll have a couple of different

walks you like to take. You don't want your outings to develop into a monotonous routine.

Dress for the weather. If it is warm, be sure to wear light, loose clothing that will allow you to cool off. In the cold, wear layers of clothes so that you can remove some if you start to get too warm. Always wear a hat in cold weather, particularly if, as in my case, the years and your heredity have robbed you of your natural protection up top. Also, use your common sense, and don't walk in extremes of temperature. You get no points for trying to be Admiral Byrd or Lawrence of Arabia.

Especially in warm weather, drink enough fluids. Eight ounces of water a half hour before starting out is a good idea. Afterward, drink to satisfy your thirst. Stick with water or fruit juice. Soda is full of useless sugar, and the so-called sports drinks offer little advantage beyond the panache of showing off to your friends what you drink. Beverages with caffeine are unacceptable as they will actually force you to urinate fluid your body wants to conserve.

AFTER YOU WALK

What you do after you're done walking may be even more important than what you do beforehand. To keep your muscles from getting tight, you should have a cool-down period and then another stretching session. The cool-down is very simple; just keep walking for a few more minutes, but at the pace of a casual stroll. Then, when you have arrived back at your starting point, go through your stretches again, just as you did after your warm-up walk.

The tendency after you're done walking will be to skip the cool-down and stretching and get back to whatever you have to do. But if you do that, you'll not only feel tight but also risk injury to the muscles.

KEEP IT SAFE

It is very unlikely that you'll hurt yourself with a walking program, but please remember that common sense is the best protection. As I emphasized earlier, check with your doctor before you start any exercise, even walking. She may have some precautions for you to follow.

There are certain warning signs that should prompt you to stop walking immediately and contact your physician. First and foremost is chest pain, especially a squeezing feeling under your breast bone. Although sore muscles and heartburn can duplicate these sensations, for our purposes chest pain comes from your heart until proven otherwise. If you experience chest pain while walking that resolves after you stop, call your doctor. If the pain persists after you stop, call your doctor immediately or get yourself to the local emergency room to be checked out.

Less urgent, but still important, is shortness of breath while you walk. This may result simply from your being overweight or out of shape. If you are a smoker, you can probably count on being short of breath when you start to exercise. All the more reason to quit smoking. Difficulty breathing can indicate other problems, and having this symptom mandates a call to your doctor.

Experiencing nausea or dizziness when you walk is also an indication that all is not right, and you will need to be checked out. Also, pain in the thighs or calves that develops after you've been walking for a while and that fades away when you rest can indicate poor circulation in the legs.

Remember, walking is supposed to be pleasurable. If, when you walk, something starts to bother you physically, it may simply mean that you are out of shape. However, it could also be an indication of a medical or orthopedic problem. Don't play self-diagnostician. Call your doctor.

One of the great pleasures of walking is that you don't have to think about it that much, but please keep in mind that you may be sharing the sidewalk or road with other folks who may not have your safety foremost in their minds. Like it or not, you'll have to pay attention to other traffic, so if you can choose less congested routes, so much the better. Remember to wear light-colored clothing, especially at night, and extra specially at twilight, when visibility is poorest for drivers. If you walk on the road, be sure your direction is against the traffic.

Concern with cars is one reason I recommend you don't wear headphones and a personal radio/cassette player when you go out. Being able to hear what's going on around you will give you an extra measure of safety. Also, one of the therapeutic things about walking is that it gives you time to clear your head or think about things or just daydream. Hard to do with heavy metal pounding in your ears.

TALK A WALK, PAL

All right, enough talk. Time for some action. And no excuses. I'll find it hard to believe if you can't make the time to devote ⅟₄₈th of your day to helping yourself feel better. I don't want to hear that you're too young, or too fat, or too out-of-shape, or too old to walk. In fact, let me tell you about an incident that happened in my office several years ago.

I was preaching a walking program to a gentleman in his early eighties who had come in for a physical. He had told me he was retired, and I presumed that although he looked rather spry, he did not get much physical activity. When I tried to tell him about the benefits of walking, he would keep interrupting me with a "but, Doc," which I would ignore. I wasn't about to take any excuses.

"Abe, a half hour a day is not too much to ask," I gently reprimanded him.

Finally, he couldn't take it anymore. "But, Bob," he protested, "why do you want to keep me down to just half an hour a day? I already walk about four hours a day!"

It turned out that in his retirement he had taken a job as a foot messenger with a Wall Street brokerage firm. He was jaunting around lower Manhattan every day. I've since learned to listen a little better.

I should have known from Abe's good health that he had to be doing something physically active. Walking was his secret. It can be yours, too. Walk to prepare for surgery. Walk to lose stress. Walk to clear your mind. Walk to take off some weight. Walk to build your heart and lungs. Walk for the pleasure of someone else's company. Walk for the solace of being alone. Walk to live longer. Walk to feel good.

IF YOU CAN'T WALK

A variety of medical problems may prevent you from walking for exercise. The most common would be arthritis in the hips or knees or poor circulation in the legs. However, there are plenty of other options available to you, so inability to walk is not an excuse for not exercising. As with walking, you should gradually work up to the point where you can do these for twenty to thirty minutes three or four times per week.

- Water aerobics: Your local Y probably offers such a program. Exercises are performed in the shallow end of a pool so that the water supports much of your body weight.

- Chair marching: Sit in a hard straight-backed chair and march in place, lifting your legs alternately. If you want to do this to music, great. John Philip Sousa, of course.

- Chair cross-overs: You can alternate marching with alternately crossing and uncrossing your legs.

- Chair-arm exercise: If you cannot use your legs at all for exercise, try using your arms. You can pump them back and forth as if you were marching or move them in front of you in a bicycling motion.

Quitting

Quitting what? You know exactly what. I hope that if you are a smoker you had the good sense to quit the moment you learned you needed surgery. Frankly, cigarettes may have been a major contributing factor to the problem that now requires surgery. Okay, no need to rub it in.

There are at least four thousand reasons to quit smoking before surgery, that being the number of chemicals in cigarette smoke. Even quitting a few days beforehand will give your lungs and body a break from those toxins. By stopping smoking, you will no longer be inhaling carbon monoxide, a poison that keeps your red blood cells from delivering oxygen to your body tissues—your heart, for instance. The nicotine you will not be taking in will not stimulate your heart to beat quickly nor your body to produce abnormal amounts of certain hormones. Furthermore, by stopping well before surgery, you will not experience the added unpleasantness of nicotine withdrawal symptoms during your recovery from surgery.

There is exactly one best way for you to quit smoking prior to surgery. Cold turkey. Just throw the cigarettes away and forget about them. Many of my patients have told me that this is exactly what they did. They often say, "As soon as I found out I had to have an operation, I just threw them out and never smoked again." Surprisingly, many of them add, "I never even missed them."

You may find that dealing with nicotine withdrawal is easier if you "embrace" the discomfort that goes along with it. That is, instead of saying: "I'm going to do this, *but* it's going to make me miserable," say, "I'm going to do this, *and* it's going to make me miserable, *but* I'm going to do it anyway."

If you just try to focus on the positive end result, your current discomfort can often seem magnified. On the other hand, if you just accept the discomfort as part of the whole picture, it's easier. Be honest with yourself: "I know I'm not going to like this one little bit, but it's what I'm going to do." This philosophy can help carry you through a difficult task.

If you don't think you can quit cold, consult with your physician. She will discuss with you alternative ways to stop. But remember, time is of the essence here. You do not have the luxury of a three-month quitting schedule. Again, my advice is get rid of the damned things. Now.

THE TWAIN SHALL MEET

Regarding diet and exercise, think of MoFoH. You want your body to be as prepared for surgery as possible, so you have the **mo**tivation. You only have to **fo**rce yourself a little to eat right and keep active, and soon you'll have developed **h**ealthy new habits. And you'll realize that, like the reports of his death, Mark Twain's health advice was greatly exaggerated. Because you will be eating what you want to, drinking what you like, and doing exactly what you'd rather.

◆——————————————————————————————

CHAPTER CHECKLIST

☐ Start eating a high-carbohydrate, low-fat, moderate-protein diet.

☐ Gradually reduce and then eliminate caffeine from diet.

☐ Get comfortable walking shoes.

☐ Start your exercise program. (Check with your doctor first.) *Gradually* build up to the point where you are exercising for twenty to thirty minutes every other day.

☐ Chuck the butts.

II

MIND-BODY PREPARATION
SCRIPTS

I think; therefore, I heal.

♦

Chance favors . . . the mind that is prepared.

—*Louis Pasteur*

Surgery favors the mind and body that are prepared.

—*Robert W. Baker*

Be prepared.

—*The Boy Scouts*

Okay. You've been feeding your body healthful food. You've been exercising your muscles, heart, and lungs. You've been strengthening your mind-body connection with self-relaxation exercises. Now your operation is a few days away, and it's time to start your final preparations for easy, comfortable, successful surgery.

The mental exercises in this section use the general mind-body preparation you've done so far as the foundation to achieve specific goals: minimal blood loss during surgery,

169

maximum comfort after surgery, rapid recovery of body functions, strengthened immunity against infection, and early exit from the hospital.

Because different types of surgery affect the body differently, the goals of preparation vary somewhat for different operations. For instance, someone having a knee repaired is not concerned with the return of intestinal function, as is someone having stomach surgery. Consequently, I am going to help you customize a script for your particular type of surgery. Your operation should fit into one of the following categories:

Brain (neurosurgery)
Eyes
Chest (lungs, aorta)
Open Heart/Coronary Bypass
Abdomen
Gynecologic (female organs)
Urologic (kidneys, bladder, prostate)
Orthopedic (bones, joints, muscles, back)
Breast
Generic (any other operation not covered above)

Chapter 6 has a script for you to record and listen to for the next few days before surgery. In addition, there are verbal suggestions to add to that music tape you are going to listen to during surgery as discussed in Chapter 3, on page 91. Chapter 7 has a script for you to start using immediately after surgery.

If you do not want to be bothered with creating your own tapes, you may order customized tapes, featuring my mellifluous voice, for each category of surgery. (See the page at the back of the book for details. We will ship by priority mail within twenty-four hours of receiving your order.)

Before you start to use your presurgical script, please read the sections that follow on the particular goals we are trying to achieve. To lessen blood loss, for instance, you first need to understand what your mind is telling your body to do. This will involve teaching you the tiniest bit about some of your body's functions. No boring lectures. I promise.

BLOOD LOSS

Some blood loss during surgery is almost unavoidable. You can minimize this loss and thereby hasten your recovery and lessen the chance you'll require a transfusion. You accomplish this by training your body to shift blood flow away from the surgical area during surgery and then restore the blood flow once the operation is over. Here's how it works.

As you know, you have thousands of blood vessels, both large and small, to carry blood from your heart to every part of your body and then back again. The *arteries* conduct blood away from your heart, and the *veins* bring the blood back to your heart to start the round trip again. Your brain exerts very precise control over the flow of blood to different parts of your body, sending more to one place and less elsewhere depending on the needs of the moment. For instance, after a meal, more blood flows to your digestive organs to transport food nutrients to the rest of your body and less blood flows to your brain, which is why you feel sleepy after a large meal.

Your brain controls blood flow by causing the smallest arteries to expand or contract in diameter, thereby bringing more or less blood to a particular area. These arteries have tiny muscles that line their walls:

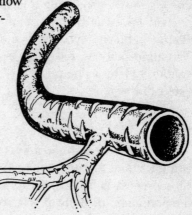

FIGURE 7

To decrease blood flow to an area, the brain sends a message down the nerves to the blood vessels' muscles, which then contract and make the artery narrower:

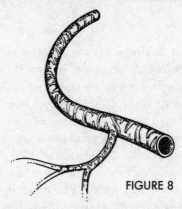

FIGURE 8

The brain can increase the blood flow by signaling the muscles to relax and expand the artery's diameter. This is exactly what happens when a person blushes. The emotion of embarrassment causes the brain to trigger a relaxation of the muscles in the blood vessels in his face. Blood pours into the opened arteries, and he turns red.

I point out blushing because it is an example of an emotion unconsciously producing a change in blood flow. What's important for us is that your mind can *consciously* produce a change in blood flow as well, and to areas other than your face. The mind-body exercises you are about to start practicing will enable you to accomplish this easily. All you have to do is listen to the tape.

INTESTINAL FUNCTION

One of your intestines' jobs is to push food, digestive juices, and gas along toward your rectum for expulsion by the body. This process is called *peristalsis*. When surgeons operate in the abdomen (or belly, if you prefer), they often have to move the intestines around. As if in protest to this manipulation, peristalsis generally shuts down for several days after surgery. If you tried to eat or drink during this time, your abdomen would become swollen and painful, and you could start to vomit. This is why, as discussed on page 96, doctors often place a drainage tube in the stomach after surgery.

Until now, there has been no way to hasten the return of intestinal function; you simply had to wait for it to recover on its own over the course of a few to several days. However, researchers at the University of California were able to accelerate the return of peristalsis by about thirty percent using simple presurgical suggestions. Their technique has been adapted for your use if you are having an abdominal operation. You will be able to start eating sooner after surgery and thereby get out of the hospital more quickly.

This picture is a schematic of your digestive tract pointing out the location of your stomach and intestines. These organs are referred to in the script, and you need to have at least a general idea of where they are.

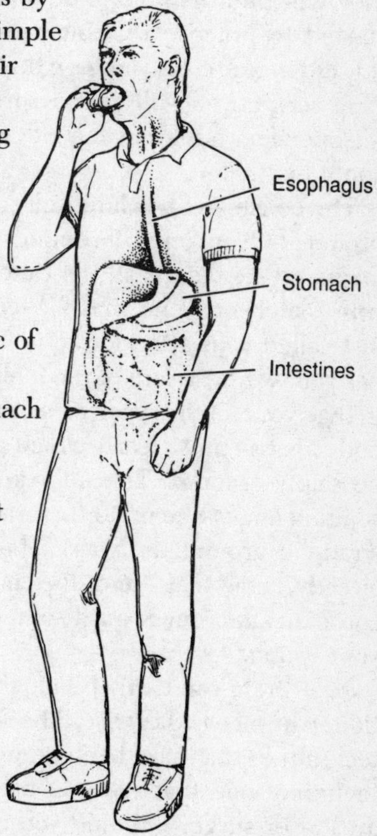

Esophagus

Stomach

Intestines

FIGURE 9

PAIN

We will take two approaches to controlling postoperative pain. The first will be to relax the muscles of the area where the surgery takes place, and the second will be to teach your mind to ignore pain so that it doesn't bother you.

One of the things that causes pain at a surgical site is contraction or spasm of the muscles in the area. Researchers have found that one effective way to combat this is to teach patients to relax the muscles of the area *before* their operations so that they will then be able to do so *after* surgery. You've already started to practice relaxing muscles consciously in the self-relaxation exercises you have been doing. (*Yes?*) In the presurgical script, you will spend some time working on relaxing the specific muscles at the site where the surgeon is going to apply his trade.

The concept of teaching your mind to ignore pain may seem bizarre to you until I remind you that your brain ignores incoming sensations all the time. At this moment do you feel your watch on your wrist? Well, you might now, since I've just called your attention to it. But up until a second ago, I'll bet you weren't aware of the feeling of your watch. The reason is that your brain receives so many inputs from all over the body that it must learn which are important and which can be safely ignored. The nerves in your wrist are continually sending a message up to the brain saying, "There's something wrapped around the wrist," but the brain in effect says, "I already know that," and does not bring the feeling into your conscious awareness until someone like me calls attention to your watch.

Your brain can easily be taught to ignore any type of sensation, painful or otherwise. The scripts employ several effective techniques that have been around for decades to achieve this, including one that you can use to mentally numb a painful area after surgery, should you need to.

IMMUNITY TO INFECTION

Now we are getting into a controversial area. It is well established that stress, including the stress of surgery, lowers immunity—your body's ability to fight off infection. Stress may do this by inhibiting the functions of white blood cells, the army of protective cells that roam your body searching out and destroying unwanted invaders.

It would therefore seem logical that if you reduce stress you should be able to improve immunity. In medicine, however, what seems logical does not always turn out to be true, and we should not assume that we can boost immune function, without having adequate research to prove it. Currently research is going on around the world investigating this question.

For this book I have reviewed the latest scientific research on the question of improving immunity by reducing stress. I think it is fair to conclude: (1) stress inhibits the body's ability to respond to infections by a number of different mechanisms; (2) reducing stress may enable immune function to return toward normal; (3) so far, no convincing studies have shown that it is possible to enhance immunity *above* normal levels.

For the practical purposes of this book, the scripts in this section seek to restore to its normal level the immunity that is suppressed by the stress of surgery.

ACCELERATING RECOVERY

Needless to say, your body tries to recover from surgery as quickly as possible. However, certain impediments to recuperation can arise during the postoperative period and delay recovery. Overcoming these impediments requires your active participation. For instance, if you do not practice deep breathing and use your incentive spirometer (see pages 94–95), you will be at risk of developing pneumonia, a definite hindrance to recovery. If you do not get out of bed soon after surgery, your muscles will start to lose their tone, and you will feel weak.

The scripts that follow will help you overcome such obstacles to recovery and even contain suggestions to help prevent potential complications that can arise from the various operations. By listening to the tapes you will both hasten your departure from the hospital and enhance your feeling of well being.

When you are listening to your tape in the hospital, you run the risk of being disturbed at any time by doctors, staff, or visitors. So I suggest you take your bedside phone off the hook and display the little sign that follows on the next page. Just tear it out of the book and put it on you or near you. Even this may not fend them off, but it's worth a try.

MEDITATING

PLEASE COME BACK

IN A

FEW MINUTES

THANKS

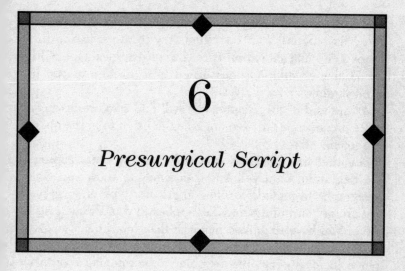

6

Presurgical Script

Depending on your particular operation, the goals of your preparation now include

- Minimizing blood loss
- Reducing and even eliminating pain after surgery
- Assisting recovery of cardiac function after heart/lung pump removal (open heart surgery)
- Hastening return of intestinal and bladder function
- Preventing suppression of immunity to infection
- Assisting wound healing
- Encouraging cooperation with breathing exercises
- Speeding recovery of mobility and muscle strength
- Enhancing the feeling of well-being
- Expediting discharge from the hospital

179

Prepare your presurgical tape and start listening to it about three days before your operation. Try to use it two to three times a day. You should prepare your postsurgical tape (Chapter 7) now as well. You may listen to it as often as you like after surgery.

At the end of this chapter you will find suggestions to add to the music tape that you are going to listen to in the operating room.

Creating your script is very easy. Simply start reading at the beginning. You will find guidelines to show you which paragraphs to include for your particular type of surgery. If you are not sure if a paragraph applies to you, throw it in! I'd rather you have too much material than too little.

To aid the return of intestinal function (after abdominal and gynecologic surgery), you are going to be thinking about your favorite food. You are also going to imagine the circumstances under which you eat it. So, for instance, if your favorite food is barbecued steak grilled in your backyard, you will visualize the steak being cooked at home and then imagine you are eating it. If your favorite food is from a restaurant, you will picture yourself in that restaurant, and so forth. When reading the script, add your own words where you see [*favorite food*].

If your operation is being performed to remove a cancer, you can add a special paragraph to the script to help relieve the emotions naturally associated with such surgery. If your surgery is not for cancer, simply skip over that paragraph as you read the script into your recorder.

To save yourself the trouble of recording your own tape, you may order one for your particular operation. (Check the back of the book for details.)

If you prepare your tape, please remember

- Read slowly and clearly in a calm, soothing voice.
- A dotted line (. . .) means pause for a few seconds.

- Instructions to be followed by the reader but not actually read aloud appear as **[boldface in brackets]**.

- Insert your first name where you see [*Your Name*]. Remember, you are speaking to yourself.

- Where you see the words [*body area*], say the name of the part of your body where you are having surgery (chest, abdomen, leg, etc.).

- Insert your own description of your "special place." There will be a line in brackets [_____] where you add your own words.

- Otherwise, read the script *exactly as written*. Every instruction and suggestion is there for a reason.

♦

All Operations

Okay, [*Your Name*], sit comfortably in your chair with your feet flat on the floor, and listen to me. Fix your attention on a spot on the opposite wall, and listen to my voice casually and effortlessly. . . . And as you look at the spot, you become aware of your breathing. Simply feel the air flowing in and flowing out. . . . Flowing in and flowing out. That's fine. . . .

On the next breath, breathe in deeply through your nose and let the breath out slowly through your mouth. **[Pause enough time to do this.]** Another deep breath in . . . and once again let it out slowly through your mouth. . . . Now a deep breath in and hold it. And as you let your breath out slowly, let your eyes drift closed. . . . Now forget about your breathing, forget about your eyes, and start to relax yourself from top to bottom.

[Read the next five paragraphs at a rate that matches how quickly you have been doing the progressive muscle relaxation. Because of your prior practice, the relaxation should proceed smoothly and quickly.]

Starting at the top of your head, feel the muscles up there, and let them go. They become heavy, limp, and relaxed. . . .

Now to the muscles of your forehead, eyebrows, and eyelids. Feel the relaxation spreading down your face. . . . Through your face, and cheeks, and jaw. As the muscles relax, your lips part a little, and this warm, pleasant feeling of heaviness starts to spread down into your body.

Feel the muscles of your neck—front and back—and let them go. . . . And the relaxation spreads down into your shoulders. Feel your shoulders sag. Notice how your arms become heavier at your sides. . . . Now the upper back muscles. Ease the tension and tightness right out of them, and let them go. . . . And down to the lower back. The muscles become very heavy, very pleasant, and very relaxed.

Now your chest muscles start to become heavy and limp. . . . And the muscles around your waist. . . . Now feel the muscles of your arms, and let them go. A feeling of heavy relaxation spreads down your arms, and they become like those two lead weights.

Now, [Your Name], the whole upper half of your body feels heavy, limp, and relaxed. And you are starting to feel very, very good. So let's go to the lower half. Feel the muscles of your buttocks and hips and allow them to relax. . . .

And this warm, pleasant feeling of heaviness spreads down into your thighs and upper legs. . . . Past your knees into your calves. . . . And all the way down your ankles and feet to the tips of your toes. So that now the leg muscles feel so heavy, limp, and relaxed that your legs also feel like two great lead weights.

Very, very good, [Your Name]. You are relaxing deeply and well, and you want to relax even more deeply. To help you, I'll count backward from ten to one. With each count you will become many times more deeply relaxed. Stress, tension, and anxiety will flow out of you, and you will feel very peaceful, very calm, and very, very good.

[During the counting, use whatever mental images help you to relax more deeply—an elevator, escalator, deep easy chair, mountain lake, etc.]

Here we go. *Ten.* Deep, pleasant relaxation. . . . *Nine.* It's nice to relax deeply. So just let it happen. . . . *Eight.* Every time I mention deeper relaxation, you go many times more deeply relaxed. . . . *Seven*. Your mind becomes like a deep, still pool. . . . *Six*. All extraneous thoughts just drift away. . . . *Five*. Going ever more deeply relaxed. . . . *Four*. All stress, tension, and anxiety are flowing out of you. . . . *Three*. Wanting to go even more deeply relaxed. . . . *Two*. Ready for the deepest possible relaxation. . . . And *One*. Deeply, pleasantly relaxed.

[Fill in the blanks in the paragraph with descriptions of your own "special place."]

Very good, [*Your Name*]. As you relax deeply and well, let's visit your special place. Remember to use all the senses of your imagination to actually experience being there. See yourself in your special place. See all the details of [_____], all the beautiful colors. . . . Hear the sounds of your special place. Hear the [_____]. . . . Feel the feelings of this wonderful place. Feel the [_____]. . . . Even smell the aromas of this place, the [_____]. Use every sense of your imagination to experience being there. And notice how very good you feel. You feel relaxed, and calm. Free from stress, tension, and anxiety. Feeling very, very good.

And you will carry this calm into your daily life and your feelings about surgery. As the day of surgery approaches, you will continue to feel calm about it. You know that you are gaining control over your mind and body, and this control will help you to come through surgery in excellent condition, free of discomfort, free of anxiety. You will make a full and rapid recovery.

All Operations Except Eyes

During and after surgery your body will respond in such a way as to enhance your success and comfort. For instance, you know that it is very important that you conserve your blood and lose as little as possible. You can accomplish this by having your body direct blood flow away from your [*body area*] during the operation. That way, there will be minimal blood loss from the surgical site.

You have already learned how words can influence the flow of blood in your body, as when embarrassing words cause more blood to flow to your face, causing you to blush. You have also learned that the blood vessels are lined with muscle cells that can contract to narrow blood vessels and direct blood away from that area in the body.

To ensure that you have very little blood loss during your surgery, it is very important that the blood move away from your [body area]. So the blood vessels in the area will contract and narrow during surgery and send the blood to other parts of your body. You will have minimal loss of blood from your [body area] during surgery because the blood vessels there will be constricted during the operation. After surgery, the blood vessels of your [body area] will open up again, allowing the blood to flow back into the area, bringing healing nutrients and oxygen to start a rapid recovery.

During your operation you will have minimal blood loss. Immediately after surgery the blood will again flow normally through your [body area], and rapid, complete healing will begin.

Open Heart or Coronary Bypass Only

During your operation, you will be placed on a heart-lung bypass machine to provide circulation to your body while you undergo heart surgery. As the operation nears its end, the surgeon will remove the machine, and your heart will be allowed to start beating again. You understand the important role your heart plays in your health and well-being, so your heart will recover quickly and start to pump with a strong, regular beat. The muscle of the heart will resume normal, healthy functioning, and you will be able to come off the machine without difficulty. Your heart will continue to pump strongly during and after your recovery period.

All Operations

Now, for a moment, return to your special place and feel completely calm. See it. Hear it. Feel it. Smell it. And feel so very good, so thoroughly relaxed.

Following your surgery you will feel very comfortable and will have minimal pain. Your mind will function in such a way that any pain signals being sent from your [*body area*] simply will not bother you. You may be aware of them, but they will be a dull, remote sensation, not painful at all.

There are several things you can do to minimize your discomfort after surgery. One of them is to relax the muscles of your [*body area*]. By relaxing these muscles, you will feel much more comfortable. So, as you come out of the operation, all the muscles of your [*body area*] will be completely limp and relaxed. With relaxed muscles in the [*body area*], you will recover more quickly and more comfortably. Therefore, all the muscles in your [*body area*] will be completely relaxed after surgery and will remain relaxed.

Let's practice relaxing these muscles right now. I am going to count *one, two, three . . . relax*. And when I do so, let all the muscles of your [*body area*] become extremely limp and relaxed. Just let the muscles go into a state of complete relaxation. Here we go: *one, two, three . . . relax*. And all the muscles go one hundred percent completely relaxed.

Now try it again. *One, two, three . . . relax*. And the muscles relax. What's interesting is that after your surgery you can perform this same exercise at any time and bring yourself rapid relief of discomfort. All you have to do is think to yourself *"one, two, three . . . relax"* and all the muscles of your [*body area*] will relax and any discomfort you have will simply fade away. Try it one more time to lock in this mind-body response. *One, two, three . . . relax*.

Here's something else you can use to relieve any discomfort you might have. Imagine next to you a large bucket of ice water. Actually see the bucket there, with all the ice cubes floating in the water, and imagine how cold that water is. Now imagine that you are dipping a washcloth into that ice water so that the cloth becomes very, very cold. In your mind, wring out the cloth and imagine you are applying it to your [*body area*]. Just feel the cloth on your [*body area*], and feel the soothing coolness penetrating through your [*body area*], numbing any unpleasant sensation.

That's right. Just imagine that your are taking a cloth, . . . dipping it into the ice water, . . . wringing it out, . . . and applying it to any area of discomfort you might have. Feel the numbing coolness penetrating your skin, so that the whole area of your body becomes pleasantly cool and numb. After surgery you will use this technique when you listen to your postsurgical tape, and you will find that it will help to provide rapid relief from any discomfort you might have.

Abdominal, Gynecologic

Now once again enjoy your special place. . . .

Because you need to eat food to bring nutrients to your body, it is important that your stomach and intestines begin to move as soon as possible after your operation. Abdominal operations cause your stomach and intestines to stop functioning for a short time. In your case, this will be kept to a minimum because you will be very relaxed and comfortable. Your stomach will pump and gurgle, and you will become very hungry soon after the operation. Therefore, your stomach and intestines will begin to move and churn so that you can eat [favorite food] soon after the operation. You will think about [favorite food] and imagine you are in [place where you eat it], and the very act of thinking these thoughts will stimulate your stomach and intestines even more to start functioning again.

Abdominal, Gynecologic, Urologic

It is also very common for bladder function to be disrupted by surgery and for it initially to be difficult for you to urinate. When you come out of surgery, there will be a catheter in your bladder to help you to urinate. Very soon, your bladder will recover its strength and tone, and when the catheter is removed, you will be able to pass your urine without difficulty. While the catheter is in, it will not bother you in the least. Very shortly after surgery, your bladder will regain its function, and you will be able to urinate normally.

All Operations

As you relax deeply and well, remember that after surgery you will be free of stress, tension, and anxiety. Because of this, your immune system will function normally. Your white blood cells will easily eliminate any infection that may arise in your body. Your incision will remain free of infection. All the cells of your immune system will work together to speed your healing and keep you free of unwanted infection.

And, [Your Name], you will heal quickly and well. Your body will call on all of its natural restorative powers to bring about rapid healing. Your surgical wound will close up tightly. You will feel good after surgery, and your body will work steadily and well to restore itself to full normal functioning.

All Operations Except Eyes

After surgery your heart will pump blood strongly, and you will fill your lungs with air to provide oxygen to all the cells of your body. You will easily and painlessly perform the breathing exercises you are instructed to do. You know that it is important to do this so that your lungs expand to their full normal state to prevent any infection from setting in. So, you will cough and breathe deeply and use your incentive spirometer. And your lungs will therefore expand fully and function normally to deliver oxygen to your blood.

Now go more deeply relaxed. You will also find after surgery that you will be eager to be up and about as quickly as possible. You will very much want to get out of bed as soon as the surgeon says you may do so. You will look forward to sitting in a chair and then walking. You know that the way to regain your strength and mobility after surgery is to push yourself a little bit, and you will look forward to sitting up and then walking as soon and as frequently as the doctors and nurses say you may. You will be pleased to do as much for yourself as you can and enjoy the feelings of increased independence and control that come with each passing day. You will look forward to your discharge from the hospital, and you will know that the more you move, the sooner you will go home.

Starting immediately after surgery you will feel very good, and with every passing day you will feel better and better. Your strength and appetite will return, and your bowels and bladder will quickly function normally. Your heart will beat strongly, and your lungs will expand fully. You will have minimal, if any, discomfort, and you will be pleased by the progress that you make. You will recover completely and quickly, and your time in the hospital will seem to pass very rapidly. Before you know it, you will be home, finishing your recuperation, feeling calm, relaxed, and very well.

Cancer Surgery Only

Cancer surgery can be a very emotional experience, but you will find that you will have feelings of optimism and calm about your operation. Fears and negative emotions will lessen, and you will look forward to making a complete recovery. Every time you practice this exercise, you will feel better and better, and you will know that your surgery will be successful and that your body will do everything it has to in order to recover completely and return to normal life.

All Operations

All these things will happen because you want them to. They will happen because of the immense power of your mind and of the mind-body connection. Your mind and body naturally want to muster all their forces to help you come through surgery and make a complete recovery. And they will. Throughout the surgical period and recuperation, you will feel calm and relaxed, free from stress, tension, anxiety, and discomfort. Also, you will feel a measure of control, because you will be an active participant in your operation and recuperation. You will come through your surgery beautifully and make a full and complete recovery.

Now, [*Your Name*], as you let these thoughts sink in and become part of the fiber of your being, return to your special place once again. Use all the senses of your imagination again to experience being there. See the [_____]. Hear the sounds of

[_____]. Feel the feeling of [_____]. Even smell the scents. And note how very good, how very calm, and how very relaxed you feel. Deeply, pleasantly relaxed.

[*Your Name*], in a few moments I am going to help you to return to your usual state of consciousness. When you open your eyes, you will feel completely calm and completely relaxed. And yet you will feel full of vibrant energy, ready to go about the tasks of the day feeling very calm, yet very energized and very good. You will know that your surgery is going to go very well, that you will be comfortable throughout, and that your body is going to heal and recover rapidly and completely.

[Pace the next paragraph to match the rate at which you like to return to normal consciousness.]

When I count to five, you will open your eyes and feel very good. *One.* Starting to return to your normal state of mind. . . . *Two.* Feel yourself lightening up. Feel energy starting to return to your arms and legs. . . . *Three.* Wiggle those fingers and toes a little to get the circulation going again. . . . *Four.* Take a deep, cleansing breath, and let it all the way out. . . . And whenever your feel ready, *Five*, you may open your eyes and feel absolutely great.

That's it! Start using this script about three days before your operation. Listen to the tape two to three times a day; it is the nitty-gritty of mind-body preparation.

MUSIC TAPE SUGGESTIONS

Drs. Carlton Evans and P. H. Richardson of Guy's and St. Thomas's Hospitals in London demonstrated that anesthetized patients who heard a tape of helpful suggestions during surgery recovered more quickly and with fewer complications than those who were played a blank tape. These patients wore special headphones to block out conversations and other sounds from the operating room.

You will be listening to music during your surgery, so you

do not need special headphones. However, you can take advantage of Drs. Evans and Richardson's research by adding your own suggestions to your music tape. You will be able to do this only if your tape player has a "Record" button and a microphone. If it does not, you can order a tape of soothing music and suggestions that I have recorded for you. (See the order page at the back of the book.)

Your music tape can be either one you record yourself or a prerecorded tape you purchase from a music store. To record over the music, you will have to put a piece of tape over the small rectangular openings on the long edge of the cassette opposite where the tape runs. Don't forget to take the tape off later so that you don't accidentally erase your music.

Record the following suggestions in a calm, soothing voice every five to ten minutes on the tape:

Everything is going very well, and you are feeling very warm, very safe, and very, very good . . . Blood is moving away from your [body area] to other areas of the body and will return when the operation is over. . . . Your heart will pump strongly and regularly. . . . After surgery you will feel calm and relaxed and have no discomfort. . . . You will have no nausea after surgery. . . . Your stomach and intestines will start to move again very soon after surgery. . . . Your bladder will function normally. . . . You will regain your strength, mobility, and appetite very quickly. You will heal rapidly and do everything you need to do to recover quickly and completely.

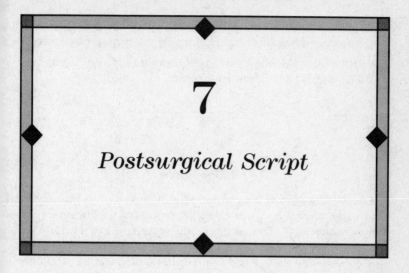

7

Postsurgical Script

You may start using this tape immediately after surgery and listen to it as often as you like. It will help you with pain relief and rapid recovery. Its goal is to help get you out of the hospital soon! Assemble this script exactly as you did the pre-surgical one, using the guidelines to select the paragraphs appropriate for your particular operation.

As you prepare your tape, please keep these things in mind:

- Read slowly and clearly in a calm, soothing voice.

- A dotted line (. . .) means pause for a few seconds.

- Instructions to be followed by the reader but not actually read aloud appear [**boldface in brackets**].

- Insert your first name where you see [*Your Name*]. Remember, you are speaking to yourself.

- Where you see the words [*body area*], say the name of the part of your body where you are having surgery (chest, abdomen, leg, etc.).

- Insert your own description of your "special place." There will be a line in brackets [_____] where you add your own words.

- Otherwise, read the script *exactly as written*. Every instruction and suggestion is there for a reason.

————————————————

◆

All Operations

Okay, [Your Name], lie comfortably in bed or sit in your chair, and listen to me. Fix your attention on a spot on the ceiling or the opposite wall, and listen to my voice casually and effortlessly. . . . As you look at the spot, become aware of your breathing. Simply feel the air flowing in and flowing out. . . . Flowing in and flowing out. That's fine. . . .

On the next breath, take a deep breath in through your nose, and let it out slowly through your mouth. **[Pause enough time to do this.]** Another deep breath in . . . and once again let it out slowly through your mouth. . . . Now a deep breath in and hold it. And as you let your breath out slowly, let your eyes drift closed. . . . Now forget about your breathing, forget about your eyes, and start to relax yourself from top to bottom.

[Read the next five paragraphs at a rate that matches how quickly you have been doing the progressive muscle relaxation. Because of your prior practice, the relaxation should proceed smoothly and quickly.]

Starting at the top of your head, feel the muscles there, and let them go. They become heavy, limp, and relaxed. . . . Now to the muscles of your forehead, eyebrows, and eyelids. Feel the relaxation spreading down your face. . . . Into your face, and cheeks, and jaw. As the muscles relax, your lips part a little, and this warm, pleasant feeling of heaviness starts to spread down into your body.

Feel the muscles of your neck—front and back—and let them go. . . . And the relaxation spreads down into your shoulders. Feel your shoulders sag. Notice how your arms become heavier at your sides. . . . Now the upper back muscles. Ease the tension and tightness right out of them, and let them go. . . . And down to the lower back. The muscles become very heavy, very pleasant, and very relaxed.

Now your chest muscles start to become heavy and limp. . . . And the muscles around your waist. . . . Feel the muscles of your arms, and let them go. A feeling of heavy relaxation spreads down your arms right to the tips of your fingers.

Now, [Your Name], the whole upper half of your body feels heavy, limp, and relaxed. And you are starting to feel very, very good. So let's go to the lower half. Feel the muscles of your buttocks and hips and let them go. . . .

And this warm, pleasant feeling of heaviness spreads down into your thighs and upper legs. . . . Past your knees into your calves. . . . And all the way down your ankles and feet to the tips of your toes. Now all the muscles of your body feel very heavy, very limp, and very, very relaxed.

Very good, [Your Name]. You are relaxing deeply and well, and you don't care much about what's going on around you. What you want is to feel good and to relax even more deeply. To help you, I'll count backward from ten to one. With each count you will become many times more deeply relaxed. Stress, tension, anxiety, and discomfort will flow out of you, and you will feel very, very good.

[During the counting, use whatever mental images help you to relax more deeply—an elevator, escalator, deep easy chair, mountain lake, etc.]

Here we go. *Ten.* Deep, pleasant relaxation. . . . *Nine.* It's nice to relax deeply. So just let it happen. . . . *Eight.* Every time I mention deeper relaxation, you go many times more deeply relaxed. . . . *Seven.* Your mind becomes like a deep, still pool. . . . *Six.* The outside world is fading away. . . . *Five.* Going ever more deeply relaxed. . . . *Four.* All stress, tension, and anxiety just flow out of you. . . . *Three.* Wanting to go even more deeply relaxed. . . . *Two.* Ready for the deepest possible relaxation. . . . And *One.* Deeply, pleasantly relaxed.

[Fill in the blanks in the paragraph with descriptions of your own "special place."]

Very good, [*Your Name*]. As you relax deeply and well, let's visit your special place. Remember to use all the senses of your imagination to experience actually being there. See yourself in your special place. See all the details of [_____], all the beautiful colors. . . . Hear the sounds of your special place. Hear the [_____]. . . . Feel the feelings of this wonderful place. . . . Even smell the aromas of this place, the [_____]. Use every sense of your imagination to experience being there. And notice how very good you feel. You feel relaxed, and calm. Free from stress, tension, and anxiety. Feeling very, very good.

As you enjoy your special place, you are making a rapid recovery from surgery. The blood vessels of your [*body area*] are relaxed and filled with blood, bringing healing nutrients to the site of your operation. The muscles of your [*body area*] are limp and relaxed, and you are free of discomfort. To help the muscles relax completely, at any time you can think to yourself "*One, two, three . . . relax,*" and all the muscles of your [*body area*] relax. Let's try it right now, "*One, two, three . . . relax.*" The muscles remain deeply relaxed, and all pain, all discomfort melt away.

You can also ease any discomfort you might have by using the cool washcloth. Right now, imagine that bucket of ice water next to you. See the ice cubes floating in the water, and imagine yourself dipping a washcloth into that ice-cold water. Now take that cold, cold cloth and apply it to your incision. Feel the soothing coolness spread into your [*body area*], numbing away any discomfort. Any pain that was there simply recedes into the background of your mind. You may be aware of it, but it does not bother you. You simply feel the cooling numbness spreading through your [*body area*]. And even after you finish the tape, you will continue to feel comfortable for many hours to come. All pain, all discomfort, simply melt away and stay away.

Open Heart or Coronary Bypass Only

During your recovery period, your heart continues to gain strength. Because of your surgery, blood is flowing more freely to and through your heart, and your heart is responding by regaining its strength. Your heart will pump strongly and regularly, healing itself to recover normal, healthy function.

All Operations

As you remain deeply, pleasantly relaxed, it would be nice to visit your special place again, so why don't you do that right now. See it. . . . Hear it. . . . Feel it. . . . Sense it in every way. And notice that you feel very peaceful, very comfortable, very much in control, and very, very relaxed.

Abdominal, Gynecologic, Urologic

While you are in your special place, I'll ask you to think for a moment about your favorite food, the food you enjoy eating more than anything else in the world. And think about the place where you eat it. Actually see yourself there. Think of [favorite food] being prepared. And now see it being served. In your mind's eye see it being placed before you. . . . Smell that fabulous aroma. . . . And now imagine that you are eating it. Taste the [favorite food]. Feel the texture of it in your mouth. As you do so, you are stimulating your stomach and intestines to start to function. They will gurgle and churn and produce digestive juices and start to move again. You know that it is very important for your digestive organs to start moving again, and by imagining yourself eating [favorite food] you are stimulating them to start up again. The more you think of it, the sooner they will start to work, and the sooner you will be able to eat it.

Abdominal, Gynecologic, Urologic, Prostate

Also, while you relax deeply and well, remember that your bladder is going to regain its function very quickly, and you will very soon be able to urinate on your own. It is possible that during your surgery a catheter was placed in your bladder to drain your urine. If so, that catheter does not bother you in any way, and in fact you are barely aware of its presence. Soon the doctors and nurses will remove the catheter, and when they do, you will be able to pass your urine on your own very promptly. You will not have any discomfort in urinating, and your bladder will quickly recover its normal strength and function.

Chest Only

As you enter the recovery period, there are several things that you can do to assist in a rapid recovery. You will easily cooperate with the nurses and doctors in performing the breathing and coughing exercises they prescribe for you, and you will very much want to do so. You will use your incentive spirometer regularly, and you will expand your lungs so that they can deliver oxygen to your blood. These exercises will help speed your recovery, and you will be able to do them despite having had surgery on your chest and despite the fact that there may be a chest tube in place. The chest tube will cause you no significant discomfort, and you will barely notice that it is there.

Also, you will find that you will very much want to get out of bed, to sit in a chair, and to walk about as soon as the doctors and nurses say you can. You will move about easily and comfortably, very quickly regaining the strength in your muscles.

All Operations Except Eyes and Chest

As you enter the recovery period, there are several things that you can do to assist in a rapid recovery. You will easily cooperate with the nurses and doctors in performing the breathing and coughing exercises they prescribe for you, and you will very much want to do so. You will use your incentive spirometer regularly, and you will expand your lungs so that they can deliver oxygen to your blood. These exercises will help speed your recovery.

Also, you will find that you will very much want to get out of bed, to sit in a chair, and to walk about as soon as the doctors and nurses say you can. You will move about easily and comfortably, very quickly regaining the strength in your muscles.

Cancer Only

At this time, please visit your special place once again. See it . . . Hear it . . . Sense it in every way. As always, visiting your special place gives you a remarkable feeling of calm and peace, free from stress, tension, and anxiety. You feel good, and you know that you will make a complete recovery. You feel optimistic and good about yourself. Negative emotions and fears simply melt away and will stay away. You know that you are going to make a complete recovery, and you look forward to resuming a normal, healthy life.

All Operations

Now once again relax deeply and well. Enjoy a pleasant feeling of calm. Free from stress, tension, anxiety, and discomfort. And because of this freedom from stress, your immune system will function at full capacity. Your white blood cells will seek out and destroy all invaders and prevent infection from setting in. All the mechanisms of healing that your body has will come into play. Your incision will heal quickly, and you will recover completely and rapidly.

All Operations

To help you achieve a rapid and full recovery, it is very beneficial to think a little catchphrase to yourself. The words are simple, yet powerful. "Day by day, in every way, I am better and better." By thinking this phrase to yourself, you will be encouraging and stimulating your body to feel better, to heal faster. Simply think the words to yourself along with me: "Day by day, in every way, I am better and better." . . . Once again: "Day by day, in every way, I am better and better." . . . And one more time: "Day by day, in every way, I am better and better."

Any time you want to, you may think this little phrase to yourself several times. And every time you do so, it will have strong healing and restorative effects on you. You will feel terrific and recover rapidly, all through the tremendous power of your own mind.

Now, [Your Name], as you let these thoughts sink in and become part of the fiber of your being, return to your special place once again. Use all the senses of your imagination again to experience being there. See the [_____]. Hear the sounds of [_____]. Feel the feeling of [_____]. Even smell the scents. And note how good, how very good you feel.

[Your Name], in a few moments you are going to return to your usual state of consciousness. When you open your eyes, you will feel completely calm and completely relaxed. Free of any discomfort. Knowing that you are making an excellent recovery from surgery.

[Pace the next paragraph to match the rate at which you like to return to normal consciousness.]

When I count to five, you will open your eyes and feel very good. *One.* Starting to return to your normal state of mind. . . . *Two.* Feel yourself lightening up. Feel energy starting to return to your arms and legs. . . . *Three.* Wiggle those fingers and toes a little to get the circulation going again. . . . *Four.* Take a deep, cleansing breath, and let it all the way out. . . . And whenever your feel ready, *Five,* you may open your eyes and feel absolutely great.

When you listen to the tape, don't forget to display your **MEDITATING** sign. You'll find it on page 177.

You now have all the tools you need to have easy, successful surgery. Keep practicing your self-relaxation and listening to your tapes right up to the time of your operation and then after it as well. Once you get home, you can read Part IV on recuperation. There you will find an additional script that will help speed along your recovery.

III

EMERGENCY SURGERY

◆

If you are having surgery in the next twenty-four hours, there is still time to prepare your mind and body to improve your outcome. If you have not already done so, please read Chapter 1 to understand what mind-body medicine is and how it can help. Next, if you have time, read Chapter 3, "The Experience of Surgery," so that you will be familiar with what you are about to go through. Then skip directly to Chapter 8, "Emergency Surgery Script," which follows this introduction.

Even if your surgery is an hour from now, just having someone read you the "Emergency Surgery Script" (or reading it to yourself) will benefit you.

After your operation, you can still help yourself with a postsurgical script to decrease discomfort and speed healing. You will find it in Chapter 7. But don't worry about this now; just remember to come back to it later.

Good luck!

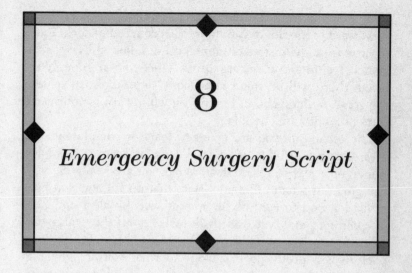

8

Emergency Surgery Script

The script that follows is a mental exercise that will both relax you and ready your mind-body connection for surgery. Having someone read you the script (or even reading it to yourself) will accomplish several things:

- Reduce anxiety about your upcoming operation
- Lessen blood loss from the surgical site
- Reduce pain after surgery
- Hasten recovery

Depending on the amount of time you have before surgery, you should perform this exercise two or three times a few hours apart. However, if there is very little time before you go to the operating room, doing it even just once will be helpful.

The exercise has six components. First, we'll do some controlled breathing. Then we will relax every muscle in your body, starting from the top of your head and working slowly downward to the tips of your toes. Next come some techniques to produce a deep state of mental calm, followed by a visualization technique to release stress. Once you are deeply relaxed, there will be some mind-body suggestions to achieve the goals outlined above. Finally, we will return to your usual state of mental functioning.

The technique you are about to learn is completely safe. There is no possibility of physical or mental harm. It is not a trance or a loss of self-control. What you are really doing is bringing out a natural mental state that up till now you have never learned to control. Your mind will be alert and fully functioning, and yet you will feel remarkably calm and relaxed.

Here is a pretty good analogy to what you are going to experience. Imagine you are sitting in a crowded room reading an absolutely fascinating book. The book is so absorbing that at times you are barely aware of the people around you. Sometimes your thoughts wander, though, and you might "tune in" to a conversation going on nearby. Soon, however, the book draws you back, and you lose yourself in it once again.

Here, instead of directing your attention to a book, you will be directing your attention inward, into yourself. At times, your thoughts may wander. That's okay. Just let those thoughts play themselves out, and then return to your self-relaxation exercise.

The most important thing to keep in mind is not to try too hard. Don't let the pressure of your current situation cause you to try to force yourself to relax. No need to think to yourself, "C'mon, relax, dammit. Let's go! Relax! Relax!" All you have to do is go through the motions, and your mind will take over. *Don't* make *anything happen; simply* let *it happen*.

Don't worry if your mind wanders as you perform this exercise. Especially don't worry if troubling thoughts come to mind. Simply let these thoughts—worrisome or otherwise—

gently float away. Some experts in meditation, such as Harvard's Dr. Herbert Benson, suggest simply thinking, "Oh, well . . ." when such thoughts intrude, letting the thoughts slip away, and then returning to what you were doing. Teachers of Transcendental Meditation suggest thinking of such thoughts as tiny air bubbles floating to the surface of a swimming pool. The bubbles (thoughts) float lazily upward, and when they reach the surface, *POP!*, they just disappear.

Just let extraneous thoughts go. Don't force them out of your mind. Let them go on their way, and then gently bring yourself back to your mental exercise.

During the exercise, you are going to be asked to make a mental journey to a "special place." It should be the most beautiful, peaceful, relaxing, secure, stress-free place you can imagine. You might want to imagine a perfect Caribbean beach, a walk through a beautiful meadow, or perhaps a favorite place from your childhood. The choice is yours. I suggest you decide on your "special place" now.

Finally, as you listen to this script, you may wonder if anything is happening. You'll feel relaxed, but otherwise not especially different from how you normally feel. Since you don't have time to read the rest of this book, you'll have to take my word for it for now: your mind-body connection will be being activated, and you will improve your surgical outcome.

You may sit in a chair or lie in bed as you do this exercise, whichever is more comfortable for you at the moment. Someone—a relative or friend—should read the script to you if possible. If no one is available, you can read it to yourself. (Just don't close your eyes where the script says to do so!) Actually read it aloud softly to yourself, mouthing the words. That will keep you from going too fast. Some things to remember as you read or as someone reads to you:

- Read slowly and clearly in a calm, soothing voice.
- Where I have put in a dotted line (. . .), pause for a few seconds.

- Where I have put [*Your Name*], insert your first name. If you are saying the script on your own, actually say your name to yourself. You are giving yourself instructions.

- Where you see the words [*body area*], say the name of the part of your body where the surgery is going to take place (chest, abdomen, leg, etc.).

- Instructions to be followed by the reader but not to be actually read aloud are put in [**boldface in brackets**].

- Please read the script *exactly as written*. Even though it may seem dull and repetitive as your read it aloud, every instruction is there for a reason. Please don't leave anything out.

◆

Okay, [*Your Name*], sit or lie comfortably in your chair or bed. . . . As you sit or lie comfortably and relaxed, pick out a spot on the opposite wall or the ceiling above eye level and look right at that spot. Just direct all your attention to that spot opposite you as you listen to me, casually and effortlessly. Just keep looking there. Good.

Now, as you continue to concentrate on that spot on the wall or ceiling, I want you to become aware of your breathing. Just become aware of the fact that you are breathing, and feel the air flowing in and flowing out. You don't have to breathe deeply or in any special way. Simply feel the air flow in . . . and flow out. That's good. You are continuing to look at the spot opposite you, but you are aware of the air flowing in . . . and flowing out.

You are going to find that as you breathe, each time you exhale, each time you breathe out, you are going to feel a bit more relaxed. That is, you will note that each time you exhale, your body will feel a bit heavier and a bit more relaxed than it did a moment before. You continue to look at your spot, but notice how a pleasant sense of heaviness is just starting to set in. [**Pause a few seconds to let this feeling happen.**]

That's good. Now on the next breath, take a deep breath in through your nose, and let it out slowly through your mouth. . . . That's good. Deep breath in, and let it out slowly through your mouth. [**Allow a few seconds for a deep, slow breath.**] Fine. And once again, a deep slow breath in through your nose, and let it out slowly through your mouth. [**Another few seconds.**] Good. Now, on the next deep breath, as you let the breath out slowly, just let your eyes drift closed. [**Few-second pause.**] Just forget about your breathing, forget about the spot you were looking at. Simply relax with your eyes closed and listen to me.

What we are going to do now is relax your body from the top of your head to the tips of your toes. The way you are going to do that is by becoming aware of different groups of muscles, relaxing them, and then forgetting about them. So right now, please become aware of the muscles on top of your head. Simply be aware of their presence. Feel them with your mind. . . .

And now, let those muscles relax. There are several ways to do this. Some people like to imagine that the muscles are getting heavy and limp. Others, that the muscles are getting rubbery and loose. Still other people like to imagine that the muscles are filling up with warm, pleasant molasses. Whatever you want to do is fine. Just feel the muscles on top of your head starting to relax. Feel the tightness flow out of them. Don't force the muscles to relax, simply *allow* them to relax. . . . That's fine. The muscles on top of your head become heavy, pleasant, and relaxed.

Now let's forget about those muscles and go down to the muscles of your forehead, and around your eyebrows and eyelids. Feel those muscles with your mind. . . . Become conscious of them. . . . Now let them relax. If you are crinkling your brow, uncrinkle it. Almost feel the wrinkles in your forehead smoothing out as the muscles there relax. Your eyelids are relaxed. They feel heavy, as if it would be an effort to open them. But you don't even want to be bothered opening them. All you want to do is let the muscles of your forehead, eyebrows, and eyelids become relaxed.

Very good. Now to the muscles of your face and cheeks and jaw. If your jaw is clenched, unclench it. Let your lips part a little. Almost imagine that you can feel the muscles of your face hanging, sagging, drooping on the bones of your face. . . . All the muscles of your face become deeply, pleasantly relaxed.

You're doing very well. This is easy, so let's go on to the muscles of your neck. Feel the neck muscles, both front and back. Be aware that we often store a lot of tension in those neck muscles. Feel if there is tightness there. Now let that tightness go. . . . Just ease it right out of those muscles. Feel the neck muscles become limp and relaxed.

Now to the muscles across the tops of your shoulders. Feel the muscles there. . . . Ease the tension and tightness right out of them. . . . And let those muscles relax. As you do so, you might notice that your shoulders sag a bit. Your arms feel a bit heavier at your sides. Because the muscles of your shoulders are becoming heavy, limp, and relaxed.

Now let's go to the muscles across your upper back, across your shoulder blades. As we go down your body, you may want to think the words along with me. In other words, you might want to think to yourself, "I can feel the muscles of my upper back. I am aware of tension and tightness there. Now I am letting that tension and tightness go. The muscles of my upper back are relaxing." Or you may simply prefer to feel the relaxation happen without thinking any words to yourself. Whichever you prefer is fine. Just ease the tension and tightness out of the muscles of your upper back, and let those muscles relax.

You may find, as the muscles of your neck, shoulders, and upper back relax, that your head wants to nod forward, or it may want to tip to one side, or it may want to stay exactly where it is. Whatever your head wants to do is fine. Just let it happen.

As we go down through your body, you might notice certain other things. For instance, you might notice a change in the pattern of your breathing. Your breathing might become slow and regular. Or you might feel a tingling in your hands, arms, or feet. Not everyone experiences these things, but if you do, just be aware that these are part of the relaxation process and don't be concerned about them.

From your upper back, let's move down to your lower back. Feel the muscles of your lower back. Feel the chair or bed pressing up against them. Now let those muscles grow limp and relaxed. . . . Deeply, pleasantly relaxed.

Okay, let's proceed now to the muscles of your chest. Feel the muscles with your mind, relax them, and forget about them. . . .

Again, as your chest muscles relax, you may notice a change in the pattern of your breathing. That's fine. Just let it happen.

From the chest down to the muscles around your waist—you're getting good at this now—just let those muscles relax and forget about them.

Now to the muscles of your arms. First feel the muscles of your upper arms, both front and back. Biceps and triceps. Good. Now let those muscles grow limp and relaxed. Let your arms grow heavy at your sides. . . . Now let this warm, pleasant feeling of heaviness go down past your elbows into your forearms. . . . And through your wrists. . . . Into your hands and all the way down to the tips of your fingers, so that now the muscles of your arms are so heavy, limp, and relaxed that your arms feel like two great lead weights that you couldn't lift even if you wanted to. But you don't even want to. All you want to do is go deeply, pleasantly relaxed.

Now, [Your Name], please notice, as you relax deeply and well, that you are aware of everything that is going on. You hear my voice. You are fully in control. You are simply allowing these things to happen. It feels good to relax deeply and well, and you would like to relax even more. So let's keep going.

Become aware of the muscles of your buttocks and hips. Feel the muscles . . . relax them . . . and forget about them.

Now down to the muscles of your thighs and upper legs. Those muscles become very heavy . . . very limp . . . and very relaxed. The heaviness and relaxation are spreading right down through you.

Okay, feel your calf muscles now. And let them relax. . . . And let the feeling of heavy relaxation spread down past your ankles, into your feet, and all the way down to the tips of your toes. So that now your legs feel like two great lead weights that you couldn't lift even if you wanted to. But, again, you don't even want to.

That's very good, [Your Name]. You've done very well. Notice that you feel relaxed and calm and completely in control. You feel very relaxed and very good, and it would be very nice to relax even more deeply. To help you do that, I'm going to count backward very slowly from ten to one. As I do, with each count, you'll feel yourself becoming more deeply relaxed. More deeply relaxed with each count, so that by the time I reach one, you will be in the deepest possible state of relaxation—completely free from stress, strain, and tension.

Here we go, now. *Ten*. It's going to be very nice to relax so deeply and so well. **[Three-to-five-second pause before saying each number.]** . . . *Nine*. It's a nice, pleasant feeling, so just let it happen. . . . *Eight*. You are allowing yourself to go ever more deeply relaxed. You might want to imagine that you are riding a long escalator or elevator down to the deepest possible state of relaxation. . . . *Seven*. Your mind becomes like a deep, still pool. A wonderful feeling of peace and calm is coming over you. Any extraneous thoughts just slip away. . . . *Six*. Imagine a beautiful mountain lake at dawn. It is perfectly still. There is not even the slightest breeze. No animals are stirring. The surface of the lake is like a perfect silver mirror. That's the complete feeling of calm that is coming over you. . . .

Five. It's wonderful to relax so deeply, and yet you would like to relax even more. . . . *Four*. Free of stress. Free of strain. Wonderfully, pleasantly relaxed. . . . *Three*. You've never been this deeply relaxed before. Your mind is deep and still. Any extraneous thoughts just drift away. And you would like to go deeper still. . . . *Two*. Approaching the deepest possible state of relaxation. . . . And *One*. Completely, totally relaxed.

That's great, [*Your Name*]. Notice the deep, pleasant feeling of calm you have. You are completely in control, but you have allowed yourself to relax so very deeply.

Right now, we're going to take a journey to the most beautiful, peaceful, relaxing place on earth you can possibly imagine. Your special place. And we're going to use all the senses of your imagination to experience actually being there. So right now, in your mind's eye, see yourself in your special place. Actually see this place in your mind. See it in great detail. Depending on where you are, see the individual grains of sand. Or single blades of grass. Or each leaf on each tree. See how beautiful it is. The colors are the most vibrant you can imagine. The sky is a beautiful, rich blue. If there is water, it is the deepest blue you have ever seen. Plants are a lush green. You can see every detail of your special place in your mind. . . .

Hear the sounds of your special place. Maybe it's the sound of waves coming gently on shore. Or a soft breeze blowing through some nearby trees. Or the familiar sounds of an old house. Or some children playing in the distance. Just hear the sounds of your beautiful, special place. . . .

Feel the feelings of your special place. Perhaps you are basking in a warm, gentle sun. Maybe there is a soft breeze blowing through your hair. If there is sand, let it run over your fingers. It feels so good to be here. Just enjoy the feelings. . . .

Even smell the scents of this beautiful, special place. The fresh ocean air. Or maybe the smell of a cool meadow. Or a deep woods. Whatever it may be, enjoy the smells of your special place. . . . If there are any tastes associated with your place, even enjoy them, too.

Experience the wonderful, relaxing calm of being in your special place. See it. Hear it. Feel it. Smell it. It's so wonderful to be here. Notice how all anxiety, stress, and strain just melt away. You feel so very relaxed, so calm. So good. Nothing is bothering you at the moment, and it's wonderful to feel so very good. . . . Just enjoy this marvelous, peaceful calm.

And, [Your Name], the best part is that this feeling of complete and total calm will stay with you even when you have completed your relaxation exercise. In a few minutes, when you return to everyday life, you will notice a wonderful sense of peace. You'll feel calm and relaxed. Any anxiety you have about your surgery will be greatly reduced, and your mind and body will function in such a way as to greatly improve the outcome of your surgery.

During and after surgery your body will respond in such a way as to enhance your success and comfort. For instance, you know that it is very important that you conserve your blood and lose as little as possible. You can accomplish this by having your body direct blood flow away from your [body area] during the operation. That way, there will be minimal blood loss from the surgical site.

Words can influence the flow of blood in your body, as when embarrassing words cause more blood to flow to your face, making you blush. This happens because the blood vessels are lined with muscle cells, which can relax, widening the blood vessels and allowing more blood to flow into the area. The reverse can also happen: the muscles in the blood vessels can contract, narrowing the blood vessels and directing blood away from that area of the body.

To ensure that you have very little blood loss during your surgery, it is very important that the blood move away from your [body area]. So the blood vessels in your [body area] will contract and narrow during surgery and send the blood to other parts of your body. You will have minimal loss of blood from your [body area] during surgery because the blood vessels there will be constricted during the operation. After surgery, the blood vessels of your [body area] will open up again, allowing the blood to flow back into the area, bringing healing nutrients and oxygen to start a rapid recovery.

During your operation you will have minimal blood loss. Immediately after surgery the blood will again flow normally through your [body area], and rapid, complete healing will begin.

Now, for a moment, return to your special place and feel completely calm. See it. . . . Hear it. . . . Feel it. . . . Smell it. And feel so very good, so thoroughly relaxed.

Following your surgery you will feel very comfortable and will have minimal pain. Your mind will function in such a way that any pain signals being sent from your [body area] simply will not bother you. You may be aware of them, but they will be a dull, remote sensation, not painful at all.

There are several things you can do to minimize your discomfort after surgery. One of them is to relax the muscles of your [body area]. By relaxing these muscles, you will feel much more comfortable. So as you come out of the operation, all the muscles of your [body area] will be completely limp and relaxed. With relaxed muscles in the [body area], you will recover more quickly and more comfortably. Therefore, all the muscles in your [body area] will be completely relaxed after surgery and will remain relaxed.

Let's practice relaxing these muscles right now. I am going to count one, two, three . . . relax. And when I do so, let all the muscles of your [body area] become extremely limp and relaxed. Just let the muscles go into a state of complete relaxation. Here we go: *one, two, three* . . . *relax.* And all the muscles go one hundred percent completely relaxed.

Now try it again. *One, two, three* . . . *relax.* And the muscles relax. What's interesting is that after your surgery you can perform this same exercise at any time and bring yourself rapid relief of discomfort. All you have to do is think to yourself, *"one, two, three . . . relax,"* and all the muscles of your [*body area*] will relax and any discomfort you have will simply fade away. Try it one more time to lock in this mind-body response. *One, two, three* . . . *relax.*

Here's something else you can use to relieve any discomfort you might have. Imagine next to you a large bucket of ice water. Actually see the bucket there, with all the ice cubes floating in the water, and imagine how cold that water is. Now imagine that you are dipping a washcloth into that ice water so that the cloth is becoming very, very cold. In your mind, wring out the cloth and imagine you are applying it to your [*body area*]. Just feel the cloth on your [*body area*], and feel the soothing coolness penetrating through your [*body area*], numbing any unpleasant sensation.

That's right. Just imagine that you are taking a cloth, . . . dipping it into the ice water, . . . wringing it out, . . . and applying it to any area of discomfort you might have. Feel the numbing coolness penetrating your skin, so that the whole area of your body becomes pleasantly cool and numb. After surgery you will use this technique when performing your mental exercises, and you will find that it will help to provide rapid relief from any discomfort you might have.

[Read the following paragraph only if the operation is on the abdominal (belly) area.]

Now once again enjoy your special place. . . . Because you need to eat food to bring nutrients to your body, it is important that your stomach and intestines begin to move as soon as possible after your operation. Abdominal operations cause your stomach and intestines to stop functioning for a short time. In your case, this will be kept to a minimum because you will be very relaxed and comfortable. Your stomach will pump and gurgle, and you will become very hungry soon after the operation. Therefore, your stomach and intestines will begin to move and churn so that you can eat your favorite food soon after the operation. You will think about your favorite food and imagine you are in the place where you eat it, and the very act of thinking these thoughts will stimulate your stomach and intestines even more to start functioning again.

[Read the following paragraph only if the operation is on the lower abdomen (pelvis), prostrate, or female organs.]

It is also very common for bladder function to be disrupted by certain types of surgery and for it initially to be difficult for you to urinate. When you come out of surgery, there will be a catheter in your bladder to help you to urinate. Very soon, your bladder will recover its strength and tone, and when the catheter is removed, you will be able to pass your urine without difficulty. While the catheter is in, it will not bother you in the least. Very shortly after surgery, your bladder will regain its function, and you will be able to urinate normally.

[Read the rest of the script regardless of the type of operation.]

As you relax deeply and well, remember that after surgery you will be free of stress, tension, and anxiety. Because of this, your immune system will function normally. Your white blood cells will easily eliminate any infection that may arise in your body. Your incision will remain free of infection. All the cells of your immune system will work together to speed your healing and keep you free of unwanted infection.

And, [Your Name], you will heal quickly and well. Your body will call on all of its natural restorative powers to bring about rapid healing. Your surgical wound will close up tightly. You will feel good after surgery, and your body will work steadily and well to restore itself to full normal functioning.

After surgery your heart will pump blood strongly, and you will fill your lungs with air to provide oxygen to all the cells of your body. You will easily and painlessly perform the breathing exercises you are instructed to do. You will know that it is important to do this so that your lungs expand to their full, normal state to prevent any infection from setting in. So, you will cough and breathe deeply and use your incentive spirometer. And your lungs will therefore expand fully and function normally to deliver oxygen to your blood.

Now go more deeply relaxed. You will also find after surgery that you will be eager to be up and about as quickly as possible. You will very much want to get out of bed as soon as the surgeon says you may do so. You will look forward to sitting in a chair and then walking. The way to regain your strength and mobility after surgery is to push yourself a little bit, and you will look forward to sitting up and then walking as soon and as frequently as the doctors and nurses say you may. You will be pleased to do as much for yourself as you can and enjoy the feelings of increased independence and control that come with each passing day. You will look forward to your discharge from the hospital, and you will know that the more you move, the sooner you will go home.

Starting immediately after surgery you will feel very good, and with every passing day you will feel better and better. Your strength and appetite will return, and your bowels and bladder will quickly function normally. Your heart will beat strongly, and your lungs will expand fully. You will have minimal, if any, discomfort, and you will be pleased by the progress that you make. You will recover completely and quickly, and your time in the hospital will seem to pass very rapidly. Before you know it, you will be home, finishing your recuperation, feeling calm, relaxed, and very well.

All these things will happen because you want them to. They will happen because of the immense power of your mind and of the mind-body connection. Your mind and body naturally want to muster all their forces to help you come through surgery and make a complete recovery. And they will. Throughout the surgical period and recuperation, you will feel calm and relaxed, free from stress, tension, anxiety, and discomfort. You will come through your surgery beautifully and make a full and complete recovery.

Now, [Your Name], as you let these thoughts sink in and become part of the fiber of your being, return to your special place once again. Use all the senses of your imagination again to experience being there. See it. . . . Hear it. . . . Feel the feelings of it. . . . Even smell the scents. And note how very good, how very calm, and how very relaxed you feel. Deeply, pleasantly relaxed.

[*Your Name*], in a few moments I am going to help you to return to your usual state of consciousness. The way we'll do this is simply by counting from one to ten. When you open your eyes, you will feel completely calm and completely relaxed. And yet you will feel full of vibrant energy, feeling very calm, yet very energized and very good. You will know that your surgery is going to go very well, that you will be comfortable throughout, and that your body is going to heal and recover rapidly and completely.

[Pause three to five seconds between counts.]

Okay. Here we go. *One.* . . . *Two.* Feel yourself starting to lighten up just a bit. . . . *Three.* . . . *Four.* Energy is starting to return to your arms and legs. . . . *Five.* . . . *Six.* You might want to wiggle your fingers and toes to get the blood circulating again. . . . *Seven.* Feeling very good, now. . . . *Eight.* Take a deep, cleansing breath . . . and let it all the way out. . . . *Nine.* Just about ready to open your eyes. . . . And *Ten*, whenever you feel ready, you may open your eyes and feel relaxed and calm, and just great.

Again, if you have some time before your surgery, try to fit in another mental practice session in a few hours. Even if you are now about to go to the operating room, know that you have activated and prepared your mind-body connection for surgery and that the mechanisms are in place for you to have comfortable, successful surgery.

Go get 'em!

IV

AT HOME

◆

Here you are at home! The surgery's over, and you are well on the way to recovery. So you're probably wondering why this book is continuing. The reason is that a friend of mine who used the techniques you have read about so far for his own operation (he was out of the hospital a *week* sooner than his doctors had predicted) called me up and said, "I miss the tapes. I'm feeling great, but I want to do more."

I realized right away what he meant. His recuperation was proceeding well, but he wanted it to be even better. Why should he stop taking advantage of his trained mind-body connection once he left the hospital? There's no reason to. This section teaches you what you can do to help get yourself back to your normal life quickly and comfortably.

So, Peter, this one's for you.

9

Recuperation

Every second of every minute of every day your body is repairing itself. Internal organs are recovering their functions. New blood vessels are growing to bring nutrients into areas where they are needed. Muscles that had been cut are healing. Nerves are regenerating. Cells called fibroblasts are producing scar tissue to strengthen your incision. Every day, in many ways, your body is working to restore normalcy.

With so much going on in you, is it any wonder that you probably feel fatigued? In fact, you probably feel more tired now than when you were in the hospital. Another reason for this is simply that you now have to do much more for yourself. The bathroom is now probably more than just a few steps away, and it's a bit of an effort to get there. Bathing is probably exhausting. Most likely your meals are not being brought to you anymore; you have to make a trip to the kitchen or dining room to eat. If you feel like eating.

I always explain to my patients that after surgery the last

two things to come back are energy and appetite. They will come, but it takes time. The mental exercises you will learn in this chapter will help them along.

Before getting to the recuperation script, let me remind you of a few things I said about recuperation in Chapter 3, "The Experience of Surgery." Remember that the course of recovery is never a straight path upward. Even at home you will have good and bad days. What happens with time is that the bad days become less and less frequent. However, don't be surprised if for some months after your operation you still have days when you lack energy or just don't feel right.

The best philosophy of recovery is to push yourself *a little bit*. There is a tendency just to want to stay in bed and rest. People have the mistaken notion that the way to regain strength is to rest. Nothing could be further from the truth. That's like saying that the way to restore your appetite is to starve yourself.

No, the way to regain strength is to push yourself *a little bit*. Your doctor has probably outlined for you what activities you may perform and when, and you should follow these guidelines. If, for instance, he says that you may take a walk, by all means do so. Don't wait until you "feel strong enough" to get up. Push yourself *a little bit* to get up. Remember MoFoH. You have the *Mo*tivation, but you must *Fo*rce yourself to act. Soon it will be a *H*abit.

The script that follows will help you to recover your strength, energy, appetite, and mobility. It will also give you a positive outlook and enable you to reduce any residual discomfort you might have. To accomplish these goals, I have incorporated a technique developed a few years ago by Dr. Harry E. Stanton of the University of Tasmania in Australia. His methods will help you to dispose of what he calls "mental rubbish" and remove any barriers to a complete recovery. As you prepare your tape, you will probably smile to yourself as you read Dr. Stanton's "garbage chute" and "wall of obstacles" techniques. The fact is that his techniques are fun, and my patients enjoy using them.

You should use this script one to two times a day at first, and then only when you need it. You may have some additional suggestions of your own that you want to incorporate into the tape. Great! Just insert them where I have indicated. Just to remind you:

- Read slowly and clearly in a calm, soothing voice.

- A dotted line (. . .) means pause for a few seconds.

- Insert your first name where you see [*Your Name*].

- Instructions to be followed by the reader but not to be actually read aloud appear as [**boldface in brackets**].

- Insert your own description of your "special place." There will be a line in brackets [_____] where you add your own words.

◆

[*Your Name*], lie comfortably in bed or sit in a chair, and listen to me. Fix your attention on a spot on the ceiling or the opposite wall, and listen to my voice casually and effortlessly. . . . As you look at the spot, become aware of your breathing. Simply feel the air flowing in and flowing out. . . . Flowing in and flowing out. That's fine. . . .

On the next breath, take a deep breath in through your nose, and let it out slowly through your mouth. [**Pause enough time to do this.**] Another deep breath in . . . and once again let it out slowly through your mouth. . . . Now a deep breath in and hold it. And as you let your breath out slowly, let your eyes drift closed. . . . Now forget about your breathing, forget about your eyes, and start to relax yourself from top to bottom.

[**Read the next five paragraphs at a rate that matches how quickly you like to do the progressive muscle relaxation.**]

Starting at the top of your head, feel the muscles there, and let them go. They become heavy, limp, and relaxed. . . . Now to the muscles of your forehead, eyebrows, and eyelids. Feel the relaxation spreading down your face. . . . Into your face, and cheeks, and jaw. As the muscles relax, your lips part a little, and a warm, pleasant feeling of heaviness starts to spread down into your body.

Feel the muscles of your neck—front and back—and let them go. . . . And the relaxation spreads down into your shoulders. Feel your shoulders sag. Notice how your arms become heavier at your sides. . . . Now the upper back muscles. Ease the tension and tightness right out of them, and let them go. . . . And down to the lower back. The muscles become very heavy, very pleasant, and very relaxed.

Now your chest muscles start to become heavy and limp. . . . And the muscles around your waist. . . . Feel the muscles of your arms, and let them go. A feeling of heavy relaxation spreads down your arms right to the tips of your fingers.

Now, [Your Name], the whole upper half of your body feels heavy, limp, and relaxed. And you are starting to feel very, very good. So let's go to the lower half. Feel the muscles of your buttocks and hips and let them go. . . .

And this warm, pleasant feeling of heaviness spreads down into your thighs and upper legs. . . . Past your knees into your calves. . . . And all the way down your ankles and feet to the tips of your toes. Now all the muscles of your body feel very heavy, very limp, and very, very relaxed.

Very good, [Your Name]. You are relaxing deeply and well, and you don't care much about what's going on around you. What you want is to feel wonderful and to relax even more deeply. To help you, I'll count backward from ten to one. With each count you will become many times more deeply relaxed. Stress, tension, anxiety, and discomfort will flow out of you, and you will feel very, very good.

[During the counting, use whatever mental images help you to relax more deeply—an elevator, escalator, deep easy chair, mountain lake, etc.]

Here we go. *Ten.* Deep, pleasant relaxation. . . . *Nine.* It's nice to relax deeply. So just let it happen. . . . *Eight.* Every time I mention deeper relaxation, you go many times more deeply relaxed. . . . *Seven.* Your mind becomes like a deep, still pool. . . . *Six.* The outside world is fading away. . . . *Five.* Going ever more deeply relaxed. . . . *Four.* All stress, tension and anxiety just flow out of you. . . . *Three.* Wanting to go even more deeply relaxed. . . . *Two.* Ready for the deepest possible relaxation. . . . And *One.* Deeply, pleasantly relaxed.

Very good, [*Your Name*]. As you relax deeply and well, let's visit your special place. Remember to use all the senses of your imagination to experience actually being there. See yourself in your special place. See all the details of [_____], all the beautiful colors. . . . Hear the sounds of your special place. Hear the [_____]. . . . Feel the feelings of this wonderful place. . . . Even smell the scents of this place, the [_____]. Use every sense of your imagination to experience being there. And notice how very good you feel. You feel relaxed, and calm. Free from stress, tension, and anxiety. Feeling very, very good.

As you relax in your special place, imagine in front of you a long garbage chute. This chute is so long that if you peer down into it, you can't see the bottom. In your mind's eye, look down into the chute and see how deep it is. So deep that nothing thrown into it could ever come back.

And into this chute you can throw any mental rubbish that you want to get rid of. Such rubbish might include negative emotions, fears, doubts, or worries. Or you might want to dump down the chute any discomfort or fatigue you might have. In fact, you can use the chute to get rid of anything that is bothering you.

Right now, take this opportunity to dispose of any mental rubbish you want to get rid of. Throw pain down the chute. See yourself removing pain from any part of your body that bothers you, and throw it down the chute. Watch it disappear into the darkness. Know that it can't come back. Throw fatigue down the chute. Or fear. You can even throw your whole operation down the chute. See the whole surgical experience in your mind's eye, wrap it up in a garbage bag, and throw it down the chute. Watch it disappear as you put it all behind you. You can get rid of anything you want to. Just throw it down the chute.

And the wonderful thing is that by doing so, when you return to your usual state of consciousness, those things you have disposed of will no longer trouble you. They will be out of your mind, and therefore out of your life. Discomfort, fatigue, negative emotions—whatever—will be gone. So go ahead, dump any things down the chute you want to, and be done with them. . . .

Now forget about the chute and relax deeply and well. Visit your special place, if you would like, and feel peaceful and calm, free of stress, tension, and anxiety. At this point imagine in front of you a barrier to success, a wall of obstacles, if you will. This wall might look like the Great Wall of China, imposing and massive. And imbedded in this wall, like huge stones, are any obstacles that might inhibit your complete healing and recovery. Such obstacles could include negative thoughts, self-imposed limitations, self-doubts, any things that stand in the way of your complete recovery.

Now see yourself breaking through this wall and emerging triumphant on the other side. The wall and its obstacles just crumble before you. Because you have the mental ability to overcome any obstacle. Nothing can stand in the way of your full recovery and recuperation. . . .

Now forget about the wall and return to your special place. See it. . . . Hear it. . . . Feel it. . . . Sense it in every way. And as you are there, see yourself as fully recovered, fully healed. See yourself returning to your normal activities, full of strength and energy. . . . See yourself enjoying a hearty meal with a healthy appetite. . . . See yourself as you like to be. Active and vigorous, completely healed, free of any discomfort or fatigue.

Seeing it and feeling it will make it happen. You will heal yourself quickly and completely. Your energy and appetite will return fully. All discomfort will fade away until it reaches a permanent zero level. And you will feel pleased by what you are able to accomplish through the power of your own mind.

Let's further these goals by thinking the little catchphrase to yourself. Simply think the words to yourself along with me: "Day by day, in every way, I am better and better." . . . Once again: "Day by day, in every way, I am better and better." . . . And one more time: "Day by day, in every way, I am better and better."

Once again, [Your Name], please return to your special place. Feel completely and wonderfully relaxed. . . . At this point you may take a few moments to give yourself any additional suggestions to achieve any goals you wish. Simply think the words to yourself. Tell your body and mind what you want them to accomplish. Repeat the suggestions three times each. I'll pause for a few moments to give you the opportunity to do this. . . .

[Pause for about fifteen to twenty seconds.]

[Your Name], you have done very well. As you let these thoughts sink in and become part of the fiber of your being, return to your special place one more time. Use all the senses of your imagination again to experience being there. See the [_____]. Hear the sounds of [_____]. Feel the feeling of [_____]. Even smell the scents. And note how good, how very good you feel.

[Your Name], in a few moments you are going to return to your usual state of consciousness. When you open your eyes, you will feel simply wonderful—calm and relaxed, yet full of vibrant energy. All the goals you set for yourself using the chute and the wall, and all the suggestions you have given yourself will come to pass.

[Pace the next paragraph to match the rate at which you like to return to normal consciousness.]

When I count to five, you will open your eyes and feel very good. *One.* Starting to return to your normal state of mind. . . . *Two.* Feel yourself lightening up. Feel energy starting to return to your arms and legs. . . . *Three.* Wiggle those fingers and toes a little to get the circulation going again. . . . *Four.* Take a deep, cleansing breath, and let it all the way out. . . . And whenever your feel ready, *Five*, you may open your eyes and feel absolutely great.

That's it. Use it and enjoy it. And when you are feeling very good after listening to this script, don't forget to say a little thank-you to my friend Peter.

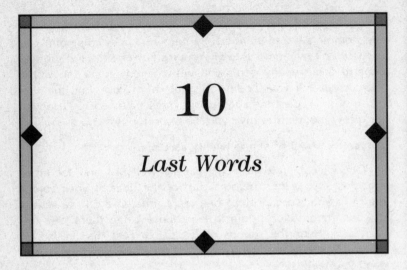

10

Last Words

I have to admit it makes me sad to write this chapter. I know I should be happy to come to the end of months of writing. But strange as it may sound, I'm going to miss you.

All through the writing of this book I have imagined you. You have been a friend and a patient whom I have wanted to help through a difficult experience. At first you were nervous, perhaps even panicky, about the idea of having surgery. So we talked about why this should be, and I explained to you what you would be going through.

I wanted you to know about the mind-body connection so that you could use it to help yourself. I was excited to impart knowledge that I knew would be useful to you for the rest of your life. As I always am with my patients, I was eager to teach you the self-relaxation exercises because I knew how much better you would feel. You were right there next to me as I recited/wrote the scripts.

I have seen you on your way to the OR and visited you in the Recovery Room afterward. I have seen you take your first steps and eat your first meal after surgery. I have watched your family or friends pick you up at the hospital and bring you home. I have shared your relief at finally being home again. I have taken joy in your recuperation and your return to normal life.

But even though we are parting ways now, I hope that you will carry the skills and lessons you have learned here with you, that you will continue to perform the mental exercises to accomplish anything you want. You'll be able to sit down, go through the steps of self-relaxation, visit your special place, and then give yourself suggestions for whatever it is you want to achieve. Without a tape. Without my being there.

I feel like a teacher who has watched his student learn and grow and excel at what was being taught. And, like a teacher, I feel the sadness of a favorite student and friend leaving and moving on.

So, good luck and good health to you. And should we ever meet, I'll look forward to shaking your hand and reliving the experiences we've just been through together.

Robert W. Baker, M.D.
c/o Successful Surgery
P. O. Box 248
Woodbury, NY 11797-2565

e-mail address:

rwbaker@ix.netcom.com

V

RESOURCES

◆

Patient Support Groups

◆

Your surgeon and hospital can put you in touch with local support groups. Contact the nursing, social work, or patient services departments in your hospital.

Several of the national organizations listed below have local branches and can offer valuable information and support to people undergoing surgery.

ABDOMINAL SURGERY

United Ostomy Association
36 Executive Park, Suite 120
Irvine, CA 92714
(800) 826–0826

Excellent support for patients whose surgery often results in the permanent wearing of a surgical prothesis to collect bodily waste (either feces or urine).

Breast Surgery

Reach to Recovery
c/o American Cancer Society
1599 Clifton Road NE
Atlanta, GA 30329
(800) ACS–2345

RtR volunteers visit women undergoing surgery for breast cancer. The volunteers are all former patients themselves.

Cancer

American Cancer Society
1599 Clifton Road N.E.
Atlanta, GA 30329
(800) ACS–2345

National Coalition for Cancer Survivorship
1010 Wayne Avenue, 5th fl.
Silver Spring, MD 20901
(301) 650–8868

Provides support for "cancer survivors and their loved ones."

Cardiac Surgery

Mended Hearts
American Heart Association
7272 Greenville Avenue
Dallas, TX 75231
(214) 705–1442

This is an organization of heart surgery patients who help others through their own surgery. They visit patients and families both before and after surgery. There are two hundred local branches of Mended Hearts.

Coronary Club
9500 Euclid Avenue
Cleveland, OH 44106
(216) 444–3690

Disseminates information for people with heart disease and who have had heart surgery.

GYNECOLOGIC (FEMALE) SURGERY

C/SEC
22 Forest Road
Framingham, MA 01701
(508) 877–8266

Counseling and support for couples anticipating birth by cesarian section.

Hysterectomy Educational Resources & Services Foundation (HERS)
422 Bryn Mawr Avenue
Bala Cynwyd, PA 19004
(215) 667–7759

Will match women undergoing hysterectomy with others who have had this procedure.

LUNG SURGERY

American Lung Association
1740 Broadway
New York, NY 10019
(212) 315–8700

General

Make Today Count
P.O. Box 6063
Kansas City, KS 66106–0063

Two hundred local groups throughout the country help cancer patients and others with life-threatening illnesses.

For more sources of help, you can consult:

White, Barbara J., and Edward J. Madara. *The Self-Help Source Book: Finding and Forming Mutual Aid Self-Help Groups.* (5th ed.) Denville, NJ: The American Self-Help Clearinghouse, 1994.

A comprehensive listing of self-help groups, this guide is available in your local library or by calling the American Self-Help Clearinghouse at (201) 625–7101.

Annotated Bibliography

◆

The following are some of the best books I have found to help you learn more about your particular surgery and mind-body medicine. Most should be available in your local library.

SURGERY AND GENERAL MEDICAL INFORMATION

Bradley, Edward L., and the editors of Consumer Reports Books. *A Patient's Guide to Surgery*. Yonkers, NY: Consumer Reports Books, 1994.

> An excellent companion to *Successful Surgery*, Dr. Bradley's book covers a number of topics that I chose to leave out, including selecting a surgeon, getting a second opinion, and negotiating fees. There are also brief discussions of different type of operations.

Griffith, H. Winter. *Complete Guide to Symptoms, Illness, and Surgery*. Tuscon, AZ: The Body Press, 1985.

> Written in an abbreviated style, this comprehensive book gives information on every operation from fingernail removal to face-lifts. Also describes briefly 520 illnesses and tells what almost 800 different symptoms can mean.

Larson, David E., M.D., editor-in-chief. *Mayo Clinic Family Health Book*. New York: William Morrow and Company, Inc., 1990. Also available in CD-ROM version.

> More generously illustrated than the Columbia tome, this book has generally brief descriptions of operations, but excellent, very understandable, explanations of the problems for which the surgery is being performed.

Stern, Edward L. *Surgery. A layman's guide to common operations*. Tarzana, CA: Lawman Press, 1988.

> An excellent little book that makes even complex operations easy to understand. Written by an anesthesiologist, it is particularly complete in describing the different types of anesthesia and monitoring used during an operation.

Tapley, Donald F., *et al. The Columbia University College of Physicians and Surgeons Complete Home Medical Guide*. Various editors. New York: Crown Publishing, Inc., 1989.

> While there is no specific section on surgery, you will find a wealth of information about whatever problem you are having surgery for. Especially useful for you will be the section on diagnostic tests and procedures.

Youngson, Robert M., M.D., with The Diagram Group. *The Surgery Book: An Illustrated Guide to 73 of the Most Common Operations*. New York: St. Martin's Press, 1993.

This is an excellent, very readable source of information about your particular operation. Not only does it describe and illustrate the various operations well, but it also answers such questions as, "What is it like immediately after the operation?" and "What are the long-term effects?" The only problem with buying this book is that you will also get information about seventy-two operations that you don't care about.

MIND-BODY MEDICINE

Some books out there promote theories or make claims that far exceed what is supported by scientific research. As philosopher Alan Ross Anderson noted, it is important to keep an open mind, but not so open our brains fall out. Therefore, I favor books with a conservative approach—one that acknowledges the current limits of our understanding of this fascinating area.

Goleman, Daniel, Ph.D., and Joel Gurin, eds. *Mind-Body Medicine: How to Use Your Mind for Better Health*. Yonkers, NY: Consumer Reports Books, 1993.

Hands-down the best book on the subject. The individual chapters are written by the leading researchers in their fields. Full of fascinating and practical information.

Moyers, Bill. *Healing and the Mind*. New York: Doubleday, 1993.

Based on Moyers's public television series, this book contains interviews with leaders in mind-body medicine. Especially interesting are sections II and III, "Healing from Within" and "The Mind/Body Connection." However, in Section IV, when Moyers goes off to China to learn about "The Mystery of Chi," his absence of journalistic skepticism is disconcerting.

Spiegel, David, M.D. *Living Beyond Limits*. New York: Times Books, 1993.

> Dr. Spiegel's pioneering work with support groups for women with breast cancer was mentioned in Chapter 1 of this book. *Living Beyond Limits* is an excellent book for anyone facing a critical illness.

FOR YOUR DOCTOR

Surgeons are naturally skeptical about mind-body medicine. If your surgeon is resistant to some of the things you want to do, such as listening to a tape in the OR, here are some articles from medical journals that he or she will find interesting.

Anderson, E.A. "Preoperative Preparation for Cardiac Surgery Facilitates Recovery, Reduces Psychological Distress, and Reduces the Incidence of Acute Postoperative Hypertension." *J. Consult. Clin. Psychol.* (1987) 55 (4):513–20.

> Patients provided information about their surgery and given "coping preparations" had easier recoveries and thirty-two percent less postoperative hypertension.

Disbrow, E.A., H.L. Bennett, and J.T. Owings. "Effect of Preoperative Suggestion on Postoperative Gastrointestinal Motility." *West. J. Med.* (1993) 158:488–92.

> Controlled, prospective trial in which patients undergoing intra-abdominal surgery were given specific instructions for the early return of gastrointestinal motility. Intestinal function returned in 2.6 vs. 4.1 days in subjects, and they were discharged from the hospital 1.6 days sooner than controls.

Evans, C., and P.H. Richardson. "Improved Recovery and Reduced Postoperative Stay after Therapeutic Suggestions During General Anaesthesia." *Lancet ii,* 8/27/88:491–93.

> Double-blind, randomized, placebo-controlled trial in which intraoperative suggestions played to subjects undergoing hysterectomies reduced hospital stay and postoperative fever.

Goldmann, L., M.V. Shah, and M.W. Hebden. "Memory of Cardiac Anesthesia: Psychological Sequelae in Cardiac Patients of Intra-operative Suggestion and Operating Room Conversation." *Anesthesia* (1987) 42:596–603.

> Well-designed double-blind study demonstrating that patients do hear what is said in the OR, despite general anesthesia.

McLintock, T.T.C., H. Aitken, C.F.A. Downie, and G.N.C. Kenny. "Postoperative Analgesic Requirements in Patients Exposed to Positive Intraoperative Suggestions." *Br. Med. J.* (1990) 301:788–90.

> Double-blind, placebo-controlled study in which women who were played positive suggestions during hysterectomies used twenty-three percent less morphine during the postoperative period.

VI

REFERENCES

◆

Ader, R., D. Felten, and N. Cohen, eds. *Psychoneuroimmunology*. (2nd ed.) San Diego: Academic Press, 1990.

Allen, K., and J. Iascovich. "Effects of Music on Cardiovascular Reactivity Among Surgeons." *JAMA* (1994) 272:882–4.

Anderson, E.A. "Preoperative Preparation for Cardiac Surgery Facilitates Recovery, Reduces Psychological Distress, and Reduces the Incidence of Acute Postoperative Hypertension. *J. Consult. Clin. Psychol.* (1987) 55(4): 513–20.

Bennett, H.L., H.S. Davis, and J.A. Giannini. "Non-verbal Response To Intraoperative Conversation." *Br. J. Anaesth.* (1985) 57:174–79.

Bennett, H.L., and E.A. Disbrow. "Preparing for Surgery and Medical Procedures." In Goleman, D., and J. Gurin, eds., *Mind-Body Medicine: How to Use Your Mind for Better Health*. Yonkers, NY: Consumer Reports Books, 1993.

Cohen, S., D.A.J. Tyrrell, and A.P. Smith. "Psychosocial Stress and Susceptibility to the Common Cold." *New England J. Med.* (1991) 325:606–12.

Disbrow, E.A., H.L. Bennett, and J.T. Owings. "Effect of Preoperative Suggestion on Postoperative Gastointestinal Motility." *West. J. Med.* (1993) 158:488–92.

Egbert, L.D., G.E. Battit, et al. "Reduction of Postoperative Pain by Encouragement and Instruction of Patients." *New England J. Med.* (1964) 270:825–27.

Evans, C., and P.H. Richardson. "Improved Recovery and Reduced Postoperative Stay after Therapeutic Suggestions During General Anaesthesia." *Lancet ii*, 8/27/ 88:491–3.

Forrest, J.B., M.K. Cahalan, et al. Multicenter Study of General Anesthesia. II. Results. *Anesthesiology* (1990) 72:262–8.

Glass, D.C., and J.E. Singer. "Behavioral Aftereffects of Unpredictable and Uncontrollable Aversive Events." *Am. Sci.* (1972) 60:457–65.

Goldman, L., M.V. Shah, and M.W. Hebden. "Memory of Cardiac Anesthesia." *Anaesthesia* (1987) 42:596–603.

Holden-Lund, C. "Effects of Relaxation with Guided Imagery on Surgical Stress and Wound Healing." *Res. Nursing Health* (1988) 11:235–44.

Holmes, T.A., and R.H. Rahe. "The Social Readjustment Rating Scale." *J. Psychosom. Res.* (1967) 11:213–8.

Jamison, R.N., W.C. Parris, and W.S. Maxson. "Psychological Factors Influencing Recovery from Outpatient Surgery." *Behav. Res. Ther.* (1987) 25:31–7.

Kehlet, J. "Postoperative Pain." In Wilmore, D.W., and M.F. Brennan, eds. *Scientific American Surgery*. Vol 1. New York: Scientific American, 1994; sec. II, ch. 12:1–12.

Kiecolt-Glaser, J.K., and R. Glaser. "Psychoneuroimmunology: Can Psychological Interventions Modulate Immunity?" *J. Consult. Clin. Psychol.* (1992) 60:569–75.

Kiecolt-Glaser, J.K., and R. Glaser. "Stress and the Immune System: Human Studies." In Tasman, A., and M.B. Riba, eds., *Annual Review of Psychiatry 11*. Washington, DC: American Psychiatric Press, 1991.

Kiecolt-Glaser, J.K., and R. Glaser. "Mind and Immunity." In Goleman, D., and J. Gurin, eds. *Mind-Body Medicine: How to Use Your Mind for Better Health*. Yonkers, NY: Consumer Reports Books, 1993.

King, G.S. "Human Nature Chart." *Med. Econ.* 20 (May 1934).

Linn, B.S., M.W. Linn, and N.G. Klimas. "Effects of Psychosocial Stress on Surgical Outcome." *Psychosom. Med.* (1988) 50:230–44.

Locke, S.E., B.J. Ransil, et al. "Effect of Hypnotic Suggestion on the Delayed-Type Hypersensitivity Response." *JAMA* (1994) 272:47–52.

Ludwick-Rosenthal, R., and R.W.J. Neufeld. "Stress Management During Noxious Medical Procedures: An Evaluative Review of Outcome Studies." *Psychol. Bul.* (1988) 104:326–42.

Manyande, A., S. Berg, et al. "Preoperative Rehearsal of Active Coping Imagery Influences Subjective and Hormonal Responses to Abdominal Surgery." *Psychosom. Med.* (1995) 57:177–82.

Manyande, A., S. Chayen, et al. "Anxiety and Endocrine Responses to Surgery: Paradoxical Effects of Preoperative Relaxation Training." *Psychosom. Med.* (1992) 54:275–87.

McLintock, T.T.C., H. Aitken, et al. "Postoperative Analgesic Requirements in Patients Exposed to Positive Intraoperative Suggestions." *Br. Med. J.* (1990) 301:788–90.

McPherson, D.S. et al. "An Internist Joins the Surgery Service." *J. Gen. Intern. Med.* (1994) 9:440–44.

Mogan, J., N. Wells, and E. Robertson. "Effects of Preoperative Teaching on Postoperative Pain: A Replication and Expansion." *Int. J. Nurs. Stud.* (1985) 22:267–80.

Mumford, E., H.J. Schlesinger, and G.V. Glass. "The Effects of Psychosocial Intervention on Recovery from Surgery and Heart Attacks: An Analysis of the Literature." *Am. J. Pub. Health* (1982) 72:141–51.

Olness, K., T. Culbert, and D. Uden. "Self-regulation of salivary Immunoglobulin A by Children." *Pediatrics* (1989) 83:66–71.

Pieper, C., A.Z. LaCroix, and R.A. Karasek. "The Relations of Psychosocial Dimension of Work with Coronary Heart Disease Risk Factors: A Meta-analysis of Five United States Data Bases." *Am. J. Epidemiol.* (1989) 129:483–94.

Robinson, P., and K. Kobayashi. "Development and Evaluation of a Presurgical Preparation Program." *J. Pediatric Psychol.* (1991) 16:193–212.

Rogers, M., and P. Reich. "Psychological Interventions with Surgical Patients: Evaluation Outcome." *Adv. Psychosom. Med.* (1986) 15:23–50.

Sime, A.M., and M.B. Libera. "Sensation Information, Self-instruction, and Responses to Dental Surgery." *Res. Nurs. Health* (1985) 8:41–7.

Spiegel, D., J.R. Bloom, H.C. Draemer, and E. Gottheil. "Effect of Psychosocial Treatment on Survival of Patients with Metastatic Breast Cancer." *Lancet ii* (1989) 888–91.

Stanton, H.E. "Ego-enhancement: A Five-Step Approach." *Am. J. Clin. Hypn.* (1989) 31:192–8.

Wilson-Barnett, J. "Interventions to Alleviate Patients' Stress: A Review." *J. Psychosom. Res.* (1964) 28:63–72.

ORDER YOUR SUCCESSFUL SURGERY TAPES NOW

To make your preparation even easier, I have professionally recorded tapes of all the scripts for you. We will ship your tapes by priority mail within 24 hours of receiving your order.

1 **Self-Relaxation: Long and Short Versions** (Chapter 2)
These exercises help you strengthen your mind-body connection. They are the essential first step in preparing for surgery.
2 **Presurgical and Postsurgical: Customized for Your Particular Operation** (Chapters 6 and 7)
Specify: Brain, Eyes, Chest, Coronary Bypass (Open Heart), Abdomen, Gynecologic (female organs), Urologic (kidneys, bladder, prostate), Orthopedic (bones, joints, back), Breast, or All Other Operations.
3 **Operating Room Music Tape**
Beautiful, soothing music by Canadian composer Fara with healing, positive suggestions to listen to during your operation. Helps reduce blood loss and lessen postoperative discomfort.
4 **Recuperation Tape** (Chapter 9)
Designed to help you recover strength, energy, appetite, and mobility as quickly as possible. Includes a BONUS SCRIPT (not in the book) to use in other areas of your life.

SPECIAL OFFER

BUY THE COMPLETE 4-CASSETTE SET OF SUCCESSFUL SURGERY TAPES A
<u>**SAVE $5.00**</u>. **PLUS RECEIVE A FREE GIFT TO HELP YOU USE THE TAPES.**

FOR FASTEST SERVICE:
CALL TODAY TOLL-FREE
1-800-747-3703.
With your Visa or MasterCard Number
or
FAX THIS FORM TO: 1-516-692-6267

OR YOU CAN MAIL THIS FORM T
Successful Surgery, Inc.
P.O. Box 248
Woodbury, NY 11797-2565

SHIPPING ADDRESS: Name _____
Address _____
City _____ State _____
Zip _____ Daytime Phone (_____)_____
Date of Surgery _____

☐	Self-Relaxation: Long & Short Versions	$9.95
☐	Pre- and Post-Surgical (Operation:)	$9.95
☐	Music Tape with Suggestions for the O.R.	$9.95
☐	Recuperation/Bonus Script	$9.95
	Sub-Total	
☐	**SPECIAL OFFER: COMPLETE SET OF TAPES + FREE GIFT—SAVE $5.00**	**$34.80**
	Sales Tax (NY Residents) 8.5%	
	Handling & Priority Mail	$ 6.00
	TOTAL	$

Method of payment: ☐ Money Order for the total amount.
Charge to my ☐ MasterCard ☐ Visa   Exp. Date: Mo. _ Yr
Card No. _____-_____-_____-_____
Signature _____

Your satisfaction is guaranteed. If, for any reason, you are not completely satisfied wi
these tapes, you may return them for a full refund. Keep the gift with our complimen

2770050

I